CONVICT FREMANTLE

CONVICT FREMANTLE

A PLACE OF PROMISE AND PUNISHMENT

MICHAL BOSWORTH

University of Western Australia Press

First published in 2004 by
University of Western Australia Press
Crawley, Western Australia 6009
www.uwapress.uwa.edu.au

Publication of this work was assisted by funding from the Western Australian
Department of Housing and Works and the Heritage Council of Western Australia.

National Library of Australia
Cataloguing-in-Publication entry:

Bosworth, Michal.
    Convict Fremantle: a place of promise and punishment.

    Bibliography.
    Includes index.

    ISBN 1 920694 33 1.

    1. Convicts—Western Australia—Fremantle—History. 2.
    Fremantle (W.A.)—History. I. Title.

994.11

Cover photograph: Former convicts Tim the Dealer, Paddy Paternoster and Jimmy
outside Castle Hotel in York, 1898. Fremantle Prison collection.
Frontispiece: Broad arrow etched in prison stone. Photo by author.

Consultant editor: Ross Haig, Perth
Designed and typeset by John Douglass, Brown Cow Design, Perth
Typeset in Palatino
Printed by Craft Print International Ltd, Singapore

CONTENTS

CONVERSION TABLE

References to weights and measures are given in the way in which they were expressed at the time, in imperial units. Conversions to the metric system are as follows:

1 acre	0.405 hectare
1 foot	30.5 centimetres
1 yard	0.914 metre
1 mile	1.61 kilometres
1 hundredweight	50.8 kilograms
1 pound	454 grams
1 quart	1.136 litres
1 gallon	4.55 litres
1 bushel	0.0364 cubic metres

Currency

Australian currency changed from pounds, shillings and pence to dollars and cents in 1966. Because of variations in currency values over time, actual conversions are difficult. At the time of the currency changeover, the following conversions applied:

1 penny (1d)	1 cent
1 shilling (1s)	10 cents
10 shillings (10s)	1 dollar
1 pound (£1)	2 dollars
1 guinea	2 dollars and 10 cents

INTRODUCTION

The history of convicts in Western Australia defines the end of transportation to Australia. Great Britain transported felons to all the colonies except South Australia during the eighteenth and nineteenth centuries. In 1829 the Swan River colony was not established as a penal settlement. It was a destination for free men and women who emigrated in search of their fortunes, hoping to carve out farms to supply the home country with fine wool and other primary products. The land was virtually given to them, but many did not thrive. Not only did they struggle to understand the intricacies of ancient soils, the devastation that poison bush could cause and the ravages of summer heat, but they failed to persuade traders and shippers that it was worth their while to stop and regularly load their produce for foreign markets. They lost their indentured workers too. Either they ventured east or themselves acquired land and turned their hands to the hoe. Labour, capital and markets were necessary for prosperity and there were years when the unhappy colonists thought none of these would come their way.

After little more than a decade of white settlement, convicts began to dribble into the colony when the first boys from Parkhurst Prison arrived in 1842. But it was not until 1850 that Western Australia became a destination for adult felons. This change coincided with the impending end of transportation to the eastern colonies, and the urgent desire among groups of West Australian pastoralists and merchants to find a source of cheap labour, and acquire some government assistance.

No female prisoners were sent to Fremantle, although nearly ten thousand men were transported there. Those who left behind a wife or children were encouraged to send for them after their release, but most families refused for one reason or another to subject themselves to the long voyage. In consequence, a disparity between the sexes grew—men outnumbering women by almost two to one. The British Government subsidised impoverished women to make the journey, and around two thousand arrived to work as servants or to find a husband. They were hardly sufficient to balance the equation.

Aboriginal people were not confined in Fremantle Prison while it remained a part of the imperial convict system. Instead they were sent to Rottnest Island, and although there was a connection between the two institutions, the story of Rottnest is separate from the history of Fremantle.

Fremantle's Convict Establishment represented a substantial investment of capital and labour by the British Government considering the relatively small size of the colony. Prison building, penal discipline, stories of people and how the convict system changed over time, are the subjects of this book.

I

SETTING THE SCENE

On 6 April 1844, in the free colony of Swan River, a teenage boy was hanged by his neck until he was dead. He was choked out of his life beside the Roundhouse in Fremantle. John Gavin had been convicted in England and sent to Parkhurst Prison for juveniles, on the Isle of Wight, when he was 12 or 13. Although sentenced to ten years' transportation, he had been 'apprenticed' on arrival in Western Australia in October 1843, so technically he was 'free' when he died. For reasons never made clear, he killed his employer's son—a crime that earned the death penalty for a boy who was probably illiterate, since he signed his name with a cross, and may not have even have known his true age. Gavin's side of the story was never reported, for he denied guilt until the night before his death, when he confessed to his appointed guardian and to a clergyman who sat with him. So slight was the condemned 15-year-old that the executioner had to add weights to his legs in order that he would die more quickly.

John Gavin's death, the first execution of a European in the colony, is long forgotten—as is much of Fremantle's history. The grimness of this past has receded into distant memory, but the city was once a prison town with prisons dominating its western and eastern approaches, prison officers drinking in its pubs and convicts shuffling through its streets. Soldiers paraded or lounged around,

The Roundhouse, listed by the National Trust and the State Register of Heritage Places, was restored after a period of neglect. *Photo by author.*

grubby children ran barefoot along the dusty paths, and horses, goats and cows grazed wherever there was a patch of green. This book relates some of the changes that came to Fremantle because of those convicts. The small number of Parkhurst boys who arrived has tempted later historians to ignore their presence, but they were like army scouts who foraged ahead of the main group. They allowed colonists and bureaucrats alike to realise that the Swan River colony could be another destination for Britain's unwanted convicted men.

If we stand at the Roundhouse, we can look down Fremantle streets, but we cannot see or smell the past. We cannot hear the cries of street vendors, or notice the fearful sweat that must have dripped from John Gavin as he was led to the scaffold. We cannot bring to mind the mixed expressions of those who watched him die. Edward Robinson, a friend transported in the same ship, walked from his Guildford workplace to the Roundhouse, so upset was he on hearing the news. Subsequently, he lost his job. Did the colonists approve this execution? Did the gallows remind residents that the colony was meant to be free from convict taint? Did the death of someone so young concern them? We cannot tell, although we know that nineteenth century settlers were accustomed to dread untimely death, which could claim them or their children through accident or illness. They were used to living under a criminal law that demanded capital punishment. Murder was repaid in this way as a lesson for other boys who might have been rebellious.

The Roundhouse, built as a prison on a rocky ridge overlooking the river, the ocean and the small village of Fremantle, was the first public building of any note in the new Swan River colony. It dominated the tiny settlement, and was the first architectural structure glimpsed from the sea, although it was rarely the first topic reported in letters back home. Having chosen a free colony, new colonists did not wish to start letters with observations of a penal system. They preferred to write about the timber, stone and brick houses, their gardens, which were quickly planted on arrival and well established a few years later, or the climate, which some people loved immediately and others hated for the discomfort it caused during the long, hot summers.

As early as 1833 the perimeters of Fremantle had been surveyed: High, Cliff, Henry, Mouat, Pakenham and Market streets, King's Square and Queen's Square were marked on paper. The new arrivals slowly built along these avenues and constructed stone walls around their plots of land in concerted attempts to control the drifting sands.

In 1833 an optimistic settler wrote home:

> Fremantle to appearance is certainly a bed of sand, but in most
> parts of the township, upon the several allotments is found a
> vein of sandstone, about two feet from the surface, in sufficient
> plenty to build a cottage on each, and to wall round the same;
> and I was much astonished, as doubtless all those who have
> visited that settlement have been (whilst others would consider
> it incredible) that the same bed of sand will produce vegetables
> such as cabbage, carrots, turnips, onions, potatoes and peas,—
> than which nothing can be finer. The radishes are superior to any
> I have ever seen, cucumbers, melons and pumpkins are grown
> to the greatest perfection, and I am of opinion, that the orange,
> lemon and vine would flourish and be productive at Fremantle
> and Perth. There is scarcely an allotment in Fremantle fenced in
> and inhabited, that has not a well of excellent fresh water from
> five to ten feet deep.[1]

Optimism wilted in the glare of summer heat when Fremantle was
a less prepossessing town. Sand and white limestone then suggested
a hostile environment that would contribute to sore eyes and
sunstroke. Gardens were minimal because of water shortages. Figs,
olives and vines could be found, but potatoes, carrots and cabbages
could not. In February 1855 a Quaker traveller, Frederick Mackie,
visited Fremantle and inquired plaintively why anyone would have
thought to make their home in this place.

Surveyor General John Septimus Roe imposed a European notion
of order on this coastal patch of sand and limestone, where Aboriginal
people were accustomed to walk, to live, to hunt, and which they
regarded as their own. Their discomfort at the arrival of the white

Limestone, which even today dominates the Fremantle streetscape, was an accessible building material for the Roundhouse and other general housing. So, too, were swamp reeds and fronds from grass trees, used in early roofs. *Photo by author.*

intruders was compounded when they saw what white law did to individuals, irrespective of who they were. During the 1830s, local leaders such as Yagan and Midgegooroo were hunted down and shot; Calyute, a Murray River man, was flogged twice, once in Perth and again in Fremantle, before a group of his relatives was ambushed and killed at Pinjarra. From 1839 to 1849, an open prison was established for Aboriginal men on Rottnest Island where separation from their land and people caused them immense suffering. It was reopened in 1855, and remained so until 1903. There was no ready understanding of the cultural worlds in which Aboriginal people lived, but there were many attempts, often ill-considered, to change them into good servants and passable farmhands.

Below the Roundhouse today you can see modern attempts to

recreate a landscape similar to that greeting the first white settlers. The sand and scattered shrubs may have looked unpromising to Europeans, but they soon established smallholdings near the village and across the river, supplying the colony's inhabitants with fresh meat, milk, vegetables and fruit. John Gavin, like many of the Parkhurst boys, was employed as an agricultural labourer, having been directed to the Pollard family farm near Pinjarra. These lads had been sent to the Swan River to fill the gap caused by too few servants but, just as they began to arrive, an economic depression hit farmers and graziers. Markets for wool and wheat slumped. Some settlers lost hope, gave up their land grants and went back to England, or moved to the eastern colonies or another new country like the United States. Desperation lurked in the hearts and minds of people who could sense no future. In 1843 Reverend John Wollaston, who lived at Picton near Bunbury, wrote bitterly in his journal:

> There is no money, and there are no markets. Flocks and herds are numerous, but these constitute mere nominal wealth in the present state of the Colony. A Gentleman may kill a sheep every week, and a Bullock every fortnight, and not be able to pay for, if he can get, a respectable Servant; much less educate his children.[2]

Five years later colonists were still bewailing their fate. As one newspaper reported, immigration could not save the colony because it was known to be 'one great man-trap'. You could fall into it, but you could not escape with ease. The Parkhurst boys had landed in a society that was small, remote, class-ridden, fearful of what the future held and likely, for all these reasons, to be cruel.

2

THE CONVICTS ARE COMING!

On 1 June 1850 Royal Engineer Captain Edmund Henderson disembarked from the *Scindian* with his wife Mary and small son Douglas. He had been appointed Comptroller General and was in charge of 75 adult male convicts, a few warders, including Thomas Dixon, who had been deputy superintendent at Millbank Prison and was to be superintendent in Fremantle, 5 non-commissioned Royal Sappers and Miners, and 50 Pensioner Guards. As this influx of people, mostly men, arrived unannounced, it found neither a reception committee nor accommodation to hand. Henderson, like many newcomers, was unimpressed by his first sight of Fremantle, even though economic conditions were beginning to improve. Very little reassured him that the colony was thriving, and he later wrote that he saw this outpost teetering on the brink of failure. Lack of roads, bridges and ports, a small population and distant markets had taken their toll. However, at the age of 28 Henderson was enthusiastic to perform well in his job, earn promotion and return to England. He rushed off a message to Governor Charles Fitzgerald (1848–55) in Perth before acquainting himself with what he deemed a fishing village. He had to find a secure building for his human freight.

Captain Daniel Scott, the town's harbourmaster, owned a warehouse that Henderson arranged to rent for £250 a year, planning

An inlaid line of brick tiles, some decorated, in this pavement near Bathers Beach traces the former shoreline leading to Scott's warehouse and temporary prison. *Photos by author.*

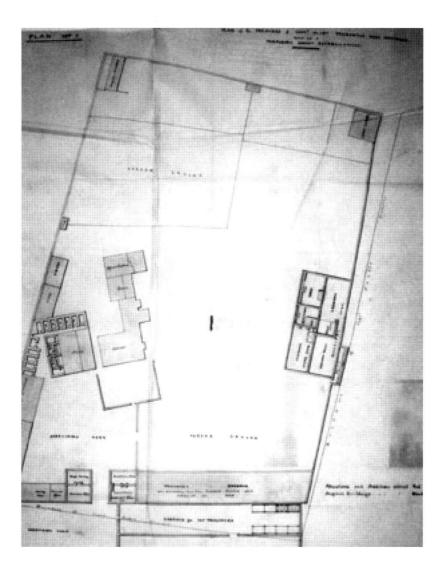

Henderson's plan of the temporary prison. *Fremantle Prison collection.*

to transform it into a temporary prison. This large shed, which became Henderson's first attempt at devising a prison, had neither windows nor timber floor, but it was not the only building on its block. Other structures were suitable for stores and accommodation. Henderson organised a party of convicts from the *Scindian* to remedy their defects. By 26 June all the men, their warders and Pensioner Guards were disembarked, and soon Superintendent Dixon was conducting tours through the prison for interested colonial observers, including the local Press:

> A few days since we visited this establishment, which we were courteously conducted over by the officer in charge. We went impressed with the idea usually entertained, of gangs of convicts working under restraint, that they would exhibit a sullen, sulky appearance, only kept to their tasks by fear of punishment, and every precaution by means of guards and sentries taken to prevent escape. What we saw was exactly the reverse; not a guard was to be seen, save a gate-keeper; not a discontented or sullen countenance was to be observed in the whole body. On the contrary, good humour, alacrity, and contentment was the characteristic of all and no person unacquainted with the fact that it was a body of convicts, could possibly have expected these fine, healthy looking men to be such, in fact we were not only surprised at what we saw but extremely gratified…[3]

Within three months the convicts had floored and reroofed the Scott warehouse, inserted windows in the walls, constructed a framework to hold the hammocks in which they slept, and provided a cookhouse, bakehouse, bathhouse, forge and privies. A storehouse, temporary hospital, rooms for warders and four strong separate cells for unruly convicts had also been built. Two long stone buildings were then hastily constructed to house as many as 360 more convicts. Everyone in the town knew just what the changes meant when a 10 foot high wall was erected around the site. Henderson hoped not only to deter would-be escapees, but also to prevent trafficking in alcohol, which was an immediate problem. Absconders were recaptured and punished.

---

16 January 1851

Prisoner 132 John Pidgeon received 50 lashes for absconding from the Convict Establishment and forfeited his ticket-of-leave. To be confined on bread and water for twelve days.

Daily routine in August 1850
5.00 a.m. 1st bell
5.15 a.m. 2nd bell, roll called
5.55 a.m. men to work
7.55 a.m. to 8.25 a.m. breakfast, grace to be said before and after
9.00 a.m. work parties out
12 midday–1.00 p.m. lunch
2.00 p.m. work parties out
6.00 p.m. stop work, parade and wash
6.15 p.m. supper
6.45–7.30 p.m. prayers
8.00 p.m. bed 9.00 p.m.[4]

Colonial Secretary's Office, Perth, September 11, 1850.

HIS Excellency the Governor directs it to be notified for general information, that any person who may be willing to engage one or more of the Convicts per *Scindian*, now at Fremantle, included in the following List, when they become entitled to Tickets-of-Leave, must make application to that effect (stating the name of the Prisoner and Trade) to the Comptroller General, at Fremantle.

By His Excellency's command,

T. N. YULE,

Acting Colonial Secretary.

Name.	Age.	Trade.	Entitled to Ticket-of-leave.	
John Dobson	30	Brickmaker	2nd Oct., 1850	
James Barker	48	Blacksmith	27th Oct., 1850	
James Morris	39	Laborer	2nd Nov., 1850	
Martin Stone	23	Groom	2nd Nov., 1850	
Robert Holder	25	Painter	3rd Nov., 1850	
Francis Westmoreland	46	Mason and Shepherd	3rd Nov., 1850	
Seymour Taylor	35	Laborer	4th Nov., 1850	General Character,—"Very Good."
Thomas Robinson	24	Stone Mason	7th Nov., 1850	
Richard Jones	37	Servant and Gardener	28th Nov., 1850	*
Frederick Ward	28	Laborer	2nd Dec., 1850	
Thomas Trott	26	Seaman	3rd Dec., 1850	
George Barker	23	Farm Laborer	3rd Dec., 1850	
Thomas R. Raine	22	Mason	3rd Dec., 1850	
John Rasan	23	Waterman	3rd Dec., 1850	
Thomas Hirst	25	Brass Moulder	3rd Dec., 1850	
Charles Pye	28	Laborer	4th Dec., 1850	
Francis Best	35	Carpenter	5th Dec., 1850	
James Sweeney	58	Ship Carpenter	10th Dec., 1850	
Samuel Diggle	37	Mason	10th Dec., 1850	
Esau Wetherall	32	Laborer	15th Dec., 1850	
Joseph Brown	37	Gardener and Groom	29th Dec., 1850	

* Engaged to His Excellency the Governor.

Ship "Sophia."

WANTED, four able Seamen for the above vessel, on wages as usual from this Port.—Application to be made to Capt CLABON, at Lodge's Hotel, Fremantle, or LIONEL SAMSON, *Agent*, Sept. 10, 1850. *Perth.*

To Brickmakers.

TENDERS will be received by Mr. J. Welbourne for making and burning 40,000 or 50,000 BRICKS in Guildford, at per thousand. The contractor to find

AT BUNBURY,—

Bunbury Lot No, 292. Upset price £10.

Wednesday, September, 25.

AT PERTH,—

Swan Location, *No.* 119—Comprising (10) ten acres more or less, adjoining the North side of Location No. 118 near N.W. angle of Perth Town Site, and in the same shape as that Location Upset price £1 per acre.

Swan Location *No.* 120—Comprising 12 acres more or less, extending 18 chains 46 links East, and 6½ chains South from the stump of a white gum tree about halfway between North ends of the Lakes Borarribup and Mariginiup, opposite boundaries parallel and equal, and all bearings true

Details of newly arrived convicts were advertised in *The Independent Journal* for the benefit of intending employers. The average age of this 1850 contingent was 33.

3

ESPLANADE PARK AND THE COMMISSARIAT

The bay that the temporary prison faced was shallow, frequently littered with seaweed and, as the port grew, the main discharge point for its rudimentary drainage system. Later it was filled with rubble, and later again metamorphosed into Esplanade Park, a focal point for families visiting Fishing Boat Harbour or Bathers Beach.

Esplanade Park was vested in the Fremantle Council in 1904.

The Esplanade and hotel in the first decade of last century. Beyond the hotel can be seen stone remains of the temporary prison. *Fremantle Prison collection and Margaret McPherson.*

Residents offended each year by the smell of rotting seaweed, and the piles of unidentifiable rubbish floating in with the tide, made their objections known. In response to the Esplanade Hotel owner, Mr A. Forsyth, and various other pressure groups, the Council decided to act and reclaim the land. The town's drains were subsequently connected to the main sewer and redirected.

To stay within an allocated budget, Council developed several stratagems. Landfill was obtained with difficulty. When it came to planting the new park, the Council saved money by acquiring couch grass from the railway reserves near North Fremantle station, mindful that the fence had to be secured each evening to prevent animals from straying on to the line. The new infilled area was carefully fertilised, using manure obtained from the cattle ships by permission of the Under Secretary of Lands. Norfolk Island pines were selected for their ability to survive the sea breezes.[5]

At the point where the coast curved inland, the colonial government granted Henderson another patch of ground. His responsibilities included establishing a prison and an administration to control the movements of convicts and goods under authority of the colonial governor. At first, all materials bound for the Convict Establishment were unloaded and stored in the temporary prison or taken upstream to a Perth warehouse. It was not long before he required a more conveniently placed building, and so convicts constructed a commissariat store, a site now occupied by the Shipwrecks Gallery of the Western Australian Maritime Museum. Tools, mattresses, clothes, paints, cooking equipment, iron, tin pots, candles, lamps, balls and chains—all were imported, listed, stored, packed, unpacked, used or sold.

Henderson, who was obliged to report on the Convict Establishment to the Secretary of State every six months, always strove to sound optimistic: 'An excellent site has been granted by the Local Government, being a position of the resumed townsite close to the water side, in every way adapted to the purpose'.[7]

In order to unload goods, the convicts built a jetty from Angelsea Point extending into South Bay. Here stores could be piled on to a wheeled vehicle that ran on wooden rails and was pushed or driven into the Commissariat's loading bay. The task of laying tramways for horse-drawn carts from jetties, quarries and the prison fell to the Royal Engineers, whose efforts reduced the hard work considerably. Despite convicts being available as a source of labour, the Royal Engineers often complained, justifiably it would seem, about a shortage of hands. It has to be remembered that some convicts disembarked with a ticket-of-leave; others had little time to serve before they earned their qualified release.

Replanted and restored shoreline looking towards the kerosene store and modern Fishing Boat Harbour, 2004. Out of sight on the left, and now some distance from the water, is the Shipwrecks Gallery. *Photo by author.*

The following are some of the goods transported by the convict ship *Lord Raglan*:

Articles for the security of convicts, including chains and basils [iron fetters and balls]
Bedding
227 coir beds
600 hammock blankets
2 surgeon's sea cots
65 sea hammocks
186 coir pillows
20 hospital sheets
clothing
cooperage stores
miscellaneous stores
6 iron sea boilers
33 hand scrubbing brushes
2 water closets
1 cover for Arms
31 table forks
4 airing stoves
9 iron ventilators
1 spittoon[6]

Men with a ticket-of-leave were permitted to work for employers in the community, earn enough to pay for their passage to the colony, and so win a conditional pardon. The ticket-of-leave men were to form a valuable labour force, especially in country areas where free men thought wages were too low.

In August 1850 convict no. 38, Charles Burgess, received the following clothes to outfit himself as a ticket-of-leave man:— jacket, waistcoat, trowser (fustian); 1 pair boots; 1 cloth cap; 2 neck handkerchiefs; 2 stockings; 2 cotton shirts; 2 flannel waistcoats; 1 serge flannel blouse; 1 leather belt and buckle; 1 pair braces; 1 bed; 1 pair blankets.[8]

By 1852 the bed and blankets were omitted from the list of articles supplied.

Between 1850 and 1868 nearly ten thousand convicts were transported. Prison warders, Royal Engineers, the 20th Company of Royal Sappers and Miners, and Pensioner Guards arrived with them.

4

THE WARDERS

The Swan River colony was to be transformed by the convicts, but not everyone was pleased with the idea of living in a penal colony. The arrival of men, presumed lawless, meant that some colonists feared they would suffer increased crime and violence in their small community unless there were sufficient means of keeping order. Others worried that lowly paid convict labour would deter poor but honest British working men from immigrating. Governor Fitzgerald recognised these points of view when he wrote to the Home Secretary noting that few free settlers would choose to emigrate to such a colony, but he could see no other means of restoring prosperity. Henderson's management had to show that those misgivings were unfounded. He had to demonstrate that the convicts were employable and, while in the prison system, sufficiently disciplined so they did not escape.

Who were the warders? Some were experienced men, previously employed in English prisons, who had accepted a free passage for themselves and family to a new life. Others were colonial-born. Not all were trained, or literate. The ability to read and write was not at first a requirement for employment, although it became one when warders needed to record the amount of labour performed by their charges and rate their prison behaviour—'poor', 'good', 'very good' or 'exemplary'. For the historian, perpetual record-keeping distinguished the convict system in Fremantle. A voluminous correspondence between the Superintendent and the Comptroller General, and the Comptroller General with officials in Perth as well as bureaucrats in London, ensured that today we have at least a formal version of events to consider. Unfortunately, few convicts or warders kept personal journals, and the letters they wrote home have mostly disappeared.

Henderson, from his lofty position in the prison hierarchy, thought many of his warders were unsatisfactory. However, those men who stuck it out and managed to find a career in the convict service were essential to his plans. Had they all decamped to the goldfields of Ballarat and Bendigo, as some undoubtedly did, transportation to the west might have proved another expensive folly of Empire. Their needs were not entirely dissimilar to his. They worked for pay, albeit considerably lower than his, a pension, subsidised food from the convict store, and accommodation.

What we see in Fremantle today, as we walk down Henderson Street, is tangible evidence of pay and conditions in the 1850s. The warders' quarters now back on to the Fremantle Markets and are surrounded by people and car parks and overlooked by pubs. When constructed, they stood as lonely sentinels on the edge of the convict grant. They showed clearly that here began an institution with rules of its own. Their very style suggested something out of the ordinary to Fremantle residents.

Henderson built three rows of terrace housing, beginning in 1851. They went up rapidly and were designed probably from a pattern book, without much thought for their tenants' comforts.

The first six houses were designed with large rooms suitable for warders with big families, who were expensive to house privately. However, the bureaucratic desire to keep costs under control was so powerful that two families were moved into each dwelling, finding themselves crowded into the space of two rooms. Fireplaces were provided only downstairs—an annoyance, since people then cooked on open fires. Henderson's plan, it seemed, reflected the attitude of a man whose meals were always prepared for him, who had little experience of noisy families (he had just one son at this stage in his life), and who was unconcerned that crowded spaces bred discomfort. Dixon pointed out to him how difficult the warders' plight was:

> The Quarters generally are ill adapted to the accommodation of two families seeing that there are fireplaces in the lower rooms only: consequently the occupants of the front room 'downstairs' whenever they wish to go 'upstairs'—have to pass through that occupied by, perhaps, another family (there being no passage to any of the houses): and the occupants of the back rooms have to pass through that occupied by the other family; thus destroying all privacy and supplying a fertile field for bickering and squabbles.[9]

Warders' quarters in Henderson Street, 2003. *Photo by author.*

The Superintendent went on to suggest that 'in the event of a warder having a large family', he might be permitted to occupy the whole house. Henderson was unwilling to allow such luxury to an employee he regarded as much beneath him, although in England warders' families generally had four rooms apiece. Instead, he eventually provided outdoor kitchens and washing places.

The second row of six terrace houses, across what is now William Street, was also designed for twelve families, but fireplaces were installed at once on both levels. These quarters had rooms so small that today one family uses the space that Henderson provided for four. The third block was constructed next to the first in 1858. Unlike the others, it has a full balcony upstairs—a later addition. These houses had flat, plain facades that were to be softened with verandas, leaving them relatively cool in summer but often damp in winter. Paint flaked from their walls, ceilings sagged, roofs leaked and until they were extended, none had a bathroom. Yet the quarters remained in use until 1991, when the prison closed. They had been repaired and improved over the years, sometimes by the tenants and sometimes with the help of prisoners.

As the number of inmates within the walls of Fremantle Prison increased, so did the number of officers, and the need for housing continued. A new row of cottages was constructed in Holdsworth Street in the 1890s when, as we shall see, the prison was overfull, and more were built close to its front wall to house female officers. But numbers also fell. In 1866, when there were fewer than 500 convicts in a prison built for more than a thousand, conditions must have improved because fewer families lived there.

Henderson's warders' quarters were certainly distinctive, but terraces never became a model for popular housing in the west. Perhaps they were too closely associated with the Convict Establishment.

While dealing with most of his employees in this way, Henderson never forgot the social layers that made up his small empire. Chief, or principal warders, were awarded another style of accommodation: four- and two-roomed duplexes. Small cottages were also constructed near the prison walls. Unlike the Henderson Street quarters, most of these smaller dwellings have been demolished. Senior officers like the superintendent, the deputy superintendent, the steward, the chaplain, the surgeon (and at a later date, the resident magistrate) lived in large homes on The Terrace in front of the prison with a wonderful view over the Indian Ocean.

In Henderson's time and later, warders preferred to live within easy walking distance of the Convict Establishment, largely because of the rigid schedule that controlled them, as much as it

The surgeon's house, 18 The Terrace, before the First World War. *Fremantle City Library Local History collection, No. 1606.*

The Gatehouse, an imposing symbol of authoritarianism separating the free from the confined. *Fremantle Prison collection.*

did prisoners. Although they worked long days, rarely less than ten hours a day and sometimes more, they were allowed fifty minutes for lunch. Those in the Henderson Street quarters could therefore look forward to walking home for the break, and be back for duty on time. They measured their day by the clock above the Gatehouse. It still chimes the hour over Fremantle.[10]

The clock, made in London in 1854 and installed two years later, was one of twelve distributed between the prison, its various buildings and the Commissariat, in that decade. They required a Mr Sweetman, who earned £24 a year in addition to his clerk's salary, to service, wind, clean and repair them. 'Telltale' clocks were later installed. They recorded the times when officers punched them in, thus acting as a check that they were performing their night routines correctly.

Warders were not well paid. During the 1860s assistant night warders, who were on the bottom rung of the ladder, earned about £30 a year, which, together with quarters, uniform and access to cheap goods from the convict store, was just about sufficient to keep one person. Wages climbed slowly even for senior officers. In 1865 a chief warder began on a salary of £112, with annual increases of £20, and principal warders ranged from £62 to £130. Dixon, whose duties were particularly demanding, because he had the responsibility of managing his staff as well as running a secure prison, had prospects of earning as much as £450, equivalent to the salary eventually paid to James Manning, the clerk of works, who started on £200. Pay rises were negotiated with the Comptroller General. Pensions were normally paid without discussion.

James Manning (1814–93), having been appointed to accompany Henderson on 7 February 1850, embarked with him on the *Scindian*, bringing his wife, two children and a servant. Manning worked long hours, supervising and designing public works where convicts were employed. He travelled to most of the sites on horseback, sometimes riding 5,000 miles a year. He retired eventually in 1872 to live in Fremantle. Perhaps because of Dr Attfield's concern in 1864 that he should replace his daily flask of brandy with one of cold tea to restore his health, he lived to make old bones.[11]

James Manning. *Fremantle City Library Local History collection,* No. 31.

Warders walked to work knowing they could not break rules or routine. They were obliged to arrive on time, to parade before the superintendent, carry keys, and be responsible for daily records of convict work and behaviour, while at the same time accepting a schedule that must have been both tiring and boring. Some drank alcohol and were fined or dismissed. Others slept their hours of night duty away and were reprimanded or fined. Some had special skills and could instruct convicts to bake bread or fabricate boots. Others, like the master tailor in 1862, were transferred because they did not reach the standards the superintendent desired. Henry Maxwell Lefroy, who succeeded Dixon in 1859, thought this man had 'very little mental ability' and was not up to the pressure of work.

Warders were also responsible for unpleasant tasks such as flogging. We know many disliked this particular job, because from time to time the superintendent was hard pressed to persuade anyone to perform it. In 1853, of the 400 lashes ordered, 148 were inflicted on seven men, the surgeon remitted 102, and 150 were remitted because no one could be found to wield the punishment. Ten years later Welsh-born warder Thomas John refused to become assistant flagellator, and instead assistant warder Harrison delivered the 100 lashes to Owen Duffy's back. John was suspended from duty. The position of flagellator was so unpopular that incentives of extra pay, up to ten shillings a flogging, or better quarters in the Gatehouse, were offered to the man who would accept the role.

The warders were exposed to a degree of danger in their job. In December 1863 John and Lane, a fellow warder, were escorting two men in the stringent discipline party back to the prison from the North Fremantle bridge where they had refused to work. The pair, John Dodd and John Holden, threatened them with crude daggers fashioned from sharpened prison spoons. Warder John disarmed them and sent his colleague for help. The two convicts were captured and put before the Superintendent, who reported to the Comptroller General that their response was the same. Each had said, 'I am tired

Henry Maxwell Lefroy (1818–79) before he became Superintendent of the Convict Establishment and father of ten children. *Fremantle City Library Local History collection, No. 314.*

of my life, I wish to be hung; if any other officers than Mr. John and Lane, who are honest straightforward men, had had charge of me, I certainly would have killed him'.[12] Punishment for this attempt was twenty-eight days on bread and water and the fastening of special 28 lb leg irons—double the usual weight. John transferred to work at the Lunatic Asylum in 1869 where he was eventually appointed principal warder in 1883. He retired in 1893, dying in 1905.

Correspondence from Superintendent Lefroy to Henderson in 1862 gives an insight to the rules that warders on night duty had to follow:

1. The charge of the lodge gates by night. This duty to be taken 'night about' by the whole of the warders on the list according to seniority.

2. The charge of the Guard room, yards and prison generally.

    The duty is taken monthly, always if practicable by a Warder, according to a regular list, but sometimes, as recently, by an Assistant-Warder, from defect of any Warder available to take it, so large a number of the Warders having now particular duties for which they possess aptitudes and from which it is undesirable to remove them for this duty.

3. Night duty in the Cellular Division and in the Hospital.

    These duties are always performed by the Assistant-Warders namely two for the Hospital and two for the Cellular Division. Each officer being on duty half the night and half the day.

    I have always been of opinion that in the Cellular Division in which all the prisoners are locked in their Cells, (and about 95 percent into Separate Cells) from which they are on no pretext whatever let out between the Evening inlocking and the Morning unlocking, except under special order from the Superintendent or Surgeon, the employment of Night Warder might safely be dispensed with, and this whole duty be discharged by Prison Constables [trusted convicts].

It is to be borne in mind that both the Hospital and Cellular Division are visited on average about once in 40 minutes throughout the whole night by the following Officers, namely the Superintendent, the Officers on Night Duty, both at the Lodge and in the Guard room: and that there is an alarm bell in the Division by which the Warder in charge can be very quickly summoned from the Guard room: and that a guard of Four Pensioners are on duty all night about the Prison inside the Walls.[13]

Group of prison officers at the end of the nineteenth century. *Fremantle Prison collection.*

Land immediately behind the Henderson Street quarters was reserved for vegetable gardens, and no doubt some families also kept hens, maybe even a pig or two. Between the gardens and the soon-to-be-constructed prison wall was an area largely unused except as a parade ground, and flanked at either end by separate barracks for the Sappers and Pensioner Guards (both long since demolished). In between, horses and other animals grazed, children flew kites, prisoners attempted to cultivate vegetables, and the warders walked to the pathway that rose from the town to the prison site. At the top, outside the Gatehouse, was a bell, only rung during emergencies. All warders, whether on duty or not, were bound to respond to its urgency.

The road which today carries traffic between Fremantle Markets and Fremantle Oval, Parry Street, was pushed through the remains of the old convict grant in the 1980s. It is probable that both Parry Street car park and the oval conceal remnants of the prison's complicated drainage system. Modernity in the form of clocks and drains arrived in town with the Royal Engineers' designs.

The Pensioner Guard parade ground with warders' quarters in background, c. 1870.
Battye Library 62188P.

One warder's life

Francis Townsend lived with his wife and ten children in a small house constructed on the north-east boundary of the prison, close to what is now Hampton Road. He began work at the prison in 1877 and remained employed for thirty-one years and eighty-seven days. It is owing to his literacy that we know as much as we do about the prison in the first years of colonial administration, since he was the Clerk in charge of records. He was sufficiently senior to be appointed acting superintendent in 1899 and again in 1906, although he was not paid extra for these more onerous duties. In May 1901 he took six weeks leave for special military duty in Melbourne with the Western Australian Contingent. He also received $7\frac{1}{2}$ months fully paid long service leave in 1906. However, when he died in 1908 he left a widow and six dependent children. She received a lump sum of £348 15s, described as a compassionate allowance, and had to find a new home.[14]

5

MILITARY EXPERTISE

The men responsible for planning and overseeing the building of the prison and its associated outposts were the Royal Engineers, an army corps whose officers never bought their commissions. They were practical, talented men who began training at Woolwich Military Academy and continued to acquire mathematics and engineering skills at the military engineering school at Chatham. During the years of peace after the end of the wars with Napoleon in 1815, some members of this officer corps had accepted senior administrative positions in the British Empire, in the absence of an alternative career path. One such man was Captain Edmund Henderson, appointed Comptroller General of the Convict Establishment after excelling in a particularly difficult survey job in Canada. He was to direct convict labour and be responsible for convict discipline. He wrote in 1853 that his duties 'which daily increase as Comptroller General of the convict department, demand all my time and exertions'. Another fully employed man was Lieutenant Henry Wray, officer commanding the Royal Sappers and Miners, who were non-commissioned soldiers. They amalgamated with the Royal Engineers in 1855. Wray also acted as Comptroller General from 1856 to 1858, and completed the prison building. His extensive responsibilities included supervising all estimates and expenditure on works throughout the colony performed by the Convict Department, a tricky assignment checked by a colonial finance committee. Two other lieutenants, Edmund Du Cane and Richard Crossman, exercised their skills outside Perth.

These men enjoyed distinguished careers when they returned to England. Henderson and Du Cane each followed Sir Joshua Jebb RE, first chairman of the Convict Prison Directorate (1850–63), into prison administration. Henderson succeeded Jebb between 1863 and 1869 before becoming Chief Commissioner of the London Metropolitan Police Force from 1869 to 1886. Du Cane, who had directed the convict depots at Guildford, York and Toodyay, was to control the convict prison system from 1869 to 1896 and was to be responsible for disengaging the Fremantle Convict Establishment from the British convict prison system in 1886. Richard Crossman, who was

initially sent to Albany to establish a prison and depot, and later was to organise other public works in rural areas, retired from the army in 1885 to stand for Parliament. Wray remained an officer, retiring in 1887 from his post as Lieutenant Governor in Jersey.

It had become clear to Henderson that a man with a ticket-of-leave was unlikely to search for employment in the underpopulated countryside, especially if he could pick up work in the towns. Convict depots were the answer. Here a man could be paid a small amount for his labour on public works while he waited for better prospects. In July 1852,

Edmund Henderson in middle age, after his return to London. *Fremantle Prison collection.*

just two years after the *Scindian* had disembarked its human cargo, Edmund Henderson made sure that the opinion of a visiting bishop from Adelaide should be related to his superiors.

> I believe this Colony must have continued to languish but for the resources of Capital and cheap labour supplied to it in this manner. Fremantle has already sprung up into a neat and thriving town: and throughout the Colony wherever the Depots have been placed, signs of industry and prosperity are apparent.[15]

Convict depots were established in North Fremantle, Mount Eliza, Toodyay, York, Bunbury, Guildford, Albany and Port Gregory. They were outstations where men under sentence, and unemployed ticket-of-leave men, were directed to work on local roads and public buildings. In Guildford Lieutenant Du Cane managed to build a bridge across the Swan River as well as repair the roads to York and Toodyay. In Bunbury and Albany the men were occupied mainly with roads and public buildings, including prisons. The depots were utilised as hiring places for ticket-of-leave men until 1856, when most were closed. By then the colonists were more accustomed to employing these men.

The 20th company of Royal Sappers and Miners began arriving in 1851 to instruct convicts in building techniques and to oversee their labour. They lived in barracks: two rooms for a married man with wife and children, and one for a single man. Henderson had requested them in his first report when he realised the extent of what had to be done, and was relieved when they disembarked, writing that 'a more valuable boon could not have been conferred to the colony'.[16] These new arrivals were to fill the roles of instructing warders and skilled craftsmen while the prison was built. They came in two groups, the first with Lieutenant Henry Wray in the *Mermaid*, and the second in the next transport with Lieutenants Du Cane and Crossman. With their presence and that of new police and water police units, Fremantle became even more of a prison town.

The presence of non-commissioned men solved the worst of Henderson's immediate difficulties. Soldiers were cheap to employ, their pay being less than a quarter that of hired tradesmen. They were well disciplined and skilled, and generally became competent teachers and reliable supervisors of convict workers. They taught men how to quarry limestone and dress it, how to make lime mortar, burn bricks, cut planks and mould the iron fittings stripped from the convict ships into bars and chains. Occasionally, some soldiers drank too much or became over-friendly with individual prisoners. The officers could restrict pay or even threaten imprisonment for such misdemeanours. The Royal Sappers and Miners were both a more reliable and a more malleable workforce than either the 'free mechanics', who could walk off the site if the going got tough, or the poorly trained convict constables.

> On 12 July 1854 Superintendent Thomas Dixon noted that the wife of Assistant Superintendent Jones at North Fremantle was investigated for 'illegally selling spirituous liquors to ticket-of-leave men: The case having been clearly proved to the satisfaction of the Magistrates she is fined in the penalty of £50'.[17] Her husband was suspended from duty, as it was believed he must have known of his wife's small business.

Pensioner Guards came out on each transport, where they maintained discipline among the convicts. They were no longer active as soldiers, but lived on a small pension from the British Treasury. Most had served in Britain's wars of invasion and conquest in places like Afghanistan, India and Africa. The colony offered a peaceful prospect of change, the hope of further responsibility in defending civilians, and even the chance of becoming a land-owner. Each man was expected to live in barracks for six months while he fulfilled his duty of mounting guard over the convicts. After this initial period, for which he received full military pay, the Guard was allowed to select an allotment of land. He might be offered anything from one to ten acres, usually in a location near an outpost of the convict department. If lucky, ticket-of-leave men would assist him to build a two-roomed cottage for himself and his family. Otherwise, he might go his own way to find other accommodation and other employment. Some sought work as prison warders. All were free settlers and, like the prison warders and Royal Engineers, also brought their families and household goods with them. Just as the warders suffered from their association with the convicts, so too did the Pensioners.

They were commanded by Captain John Bruce, who had arrived on the second convict transport, the *Hashemy*, and whose job it was to ensure the fulfilment of the contract made between the Pensioners and the colonial government.

> Mrs Janet Millett, a clergyman's wife, observed in her memoir ***An Australian Parsonage,*** written during the 1860s, that 'Between pensioners and convicts existed a very rancorous feeling, originating no doubt in the relative positions occupied by the two classes on board ship; the convicts protesting that the pensioners were quite as bad as themselves, only that they had not been found out, an assertion no ways weakened by the drunken habits in which some of the old soldiers were apt to indulge, and by the very low character of the women that many of them had married'.[18]

Recently restored Bassendean Pensioner Guard cottage, one of four built near Guildford in the 1850s. *Photo by author.*

If a Guard and his family stayed on his land and improved it for a period of seven years, it was granted to him and his heirs free of charge. Their cottages were arranged in small groups near the prison or penal depots. Especially notable was the village in North Fremantle where, by May 1854, nineteen two-roomed stone cottages, each on an acre of land, had been completed. A memory of this settlement remained for some years in Pensioner Road, now renamed John Street. Pensioner cottages were also constructed at Freshwater Bay, Bunbury, Guildford, Kojonup and Port Gregory, and some thatched rammed earth houses were provided for the Guards at outposts like York, where Mrs Millett met them, and Toodyay, although floods later swept these away. The Guards were poorly paid and appreciated access to the convict store.

Colonial food prices were considered high. Captain Bruce reported in June 1852 that meat was 8 pence and bread 3 pence a pound; potatoes were from 14 shillings to 16 shillings a hundredweight; milk was 6 pence a quart, fowls 5 shillings a pair, eggs 3 shillings a dozen and fresh butter was unobtainable—they had to make do with salted butter. In January 1860 rations were replaced by an allowance—£20 for food and £5 for fuel.[19]

The presence of the Pensioner Guards implied a message to doubtful settlers: their colony would not be destroyed by its acceptance of convicts. The former soldiers paraded and mounted guard at various places (especially in Fremantle) and wore uniform. A substantial brick barracks was to be constructed for them and their families in Perth at the head of St Georges Terrace. Only the entry arch now remains, standing as a potent reminder of imperial power.

The Pensioner Guards had taken an imaginative step in their careers when they accepted a free passage to a new penal colony, but they were men who had few resources other than the work they had known. None was independently wealthy, and most found the transition to the colony difficult and less rewarding than they had hoped. Over-indulgence in alcohol, a common colonial remedy for all manner of ills, was treated by Bruce with disdain and with discipline. Perhaps the Pensioners shared something with the convicts, who were more likely to be returned to prison because of drunkenness than for any other breach of conduct. Yet it has been suggested that the more successful Pensioners acted as a role model for those who inhabited a social strata well below them. A study of the Freshwater Bay Guards settlement found that their army training stimulated them to be resourceful and practical, qualities appreciated in a remote settlement. Given the nature of colonial society, which now was further divided into free and bond, the Guards would always have received more respect than the former felons.

In 1853 the Secretary of State advised Governor Fitzgerald that, in his opinion, the numbers of newly arrived free and convicted new settlers were just about even. The colony had not been flooded with felons. But this self-congratulatory note was a little premature. The Royal Engineers and most of the Royal Sappers and Miners were to return to England, and many of the Pensioner Guards also departed. In 1868 Bruce reported that, of the 1,191 Pensioner Guards who had emigrated to the colony, only 581 remained. Of these, 139 families were settled on the land, but 31 of this group were trying to sell up and move on.

Fremantle Oval c. 1910 was once the Pensioner Guard parade ground. In the background can be seen the barracks, later demolished to make way for hospital extensions. *Fremantle City Library Local History collection, No. 557.*

6

PRISON DESIGN

Henderson thought carefully about the right place to build the permanent prison. He was instructed by his superior in London, Joshua Jebb, designer of several prisons that reflected contemporary reforming ideas about criminal justice, to find a healthy, airy location where convicts could work for the colony. By September 1850 Henderson had selected a slope bordering the surveyed eastern boundary of Fremantle. In October 1851 Governor Fitzgerald, himself rather uneasy at the presence of so many convicts, proclaimed nearly 40 acres for the new establishment. The grant included land for the warders' quarters, barracks, grazing areas for horses and all the other buildings required by the administration.

Henderson wrote to his superiors:

> The site proposed is in every way well suited for the purpose; it is a healthy and elevated spot—removed from the business part of town, and within convenient distance of the harbour; in the improvement of which there will be employment for the Prisoners for many years after the Government works are complete.[20]

Designing a prison was not something Edmund Henderson could do from a pattern book. Prisons were buildings with more than one purpose. They had to confine and punish, but imprisonment was also meant to redeem or improve the individual. How could this be shown in a building?

Henderson drew two plans for the new prison and sent them to London for comment. Each proposed a building that was big by colonial standards, but the first, which was rejected, was based on Pentonville, the 'model prison' designed and built by Jebb in 1842. Pentonville's cells were large because the inmates spent most of their time inside them, working or studying the Bible, supposedly trying to improve themselves. An hour's exercise outside walking silently behind other prisoners was the only occasion a man saw any person who was not in authority. The prison chapel was equipped with individual seats, each divided from the next by a high partition. Everyone's attention was drawn to the pulpit, because no one could see anyone else. This regime of semi-solitary confinement was called the 'separate system' and was expected to alter the individual's outlook on life; it was hoped that by seeing the error of his ways, he would change them.

A version of the model prison was constructed at Port Arthur in Van Diemen's Land. However, prison administrators found that long periods of deprivation sent some inmates into deep depression. 'Weak-minded' prisoners were the bane of the medical men. They were rarely cured of their mental illness and many would end their days in an asylum. After serving months in the separate system, the convicts were transferred to another prison where they joined others to work on large public works, like harbour moles or drainage dykes.

Henderson was instructed to build a prison that would house men at this second stage of their punishment, and his second plan, drawn in 1851, fulfilled this directive. Now the cells could be much smaller, because the men were accommodated there only at night.

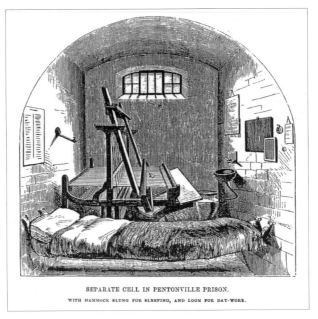

SEPARATE CELL IN PENTONVILLE PRISON.
WITH HAMMOCK SLUNG FOR SLEEPING, AND LOOM FOR DAY-WORK.

A Pentonville cell designed by Joshua Jebb.

During the day most of them were to be employed outside, creating a colonial infrastructure of roads, bridges, jetties, culverts, other prisons, warders' quarters, barracks and Pensioner Guard cottages. The cell block was planned to hold more than a thousand inmates. It was to be plain and functional, and not too expensive.

The cheapest available building material in Fremantle was limestone, so it was used throughout the complex. The convicts took six years to complete their prison, with its walls and subsidiary buildings. This was longer than the colonists thought desirable, but the labour force was far from uniform, and even nature was far from kind. In 1856 a 'whirlwind' (so described by Wray, who witnessed it) swirled from the sea and up the slope, dislodging more than 150 yards of the northern boundary wall, as well as knocking down chimneys and whipping off pieces of roof. Wray, then in charge, ordered that the perimeter wall, when rebuilt, be reinforced with columns on the inside. Prisons generally do not favour walls buttressed in this way for fear that inmates might scale them. But Wray was evidently less concerned about this possibility than he was about the likelihood of another fierce wind.

As he was responsible for the cost estimates, Wray had a bit of explaining to do in 1857 when it was clear that his budget had overrun—chiefly because the prison was 12 feet longer than he expected. He had lacked a theodolite when surveying the imperfectly cleared site and built an extra 6 feet on the southern side. The chapel was in the centre of the prison and so he had to lengthen the northern half by 6 feet to keep the symmetry we see today. As a means of minimising this error, Wray commented that he hoped he had increased the accommodation.

7

BUILDING TECHNOLOGY

Fremantle Prison was constructed of stone quarried largely from the hillside on which it stands. When that source proved insufficient, quarries around the town, including one below Arthur Head, were exploited for the building. So much stone was extracted from Fremantle during these years that the landscape was considerably altered. Only one place within the prison grounds remains to show something of the hill that was dug away—the south knoll.

South knoll over the front parade ground. *Photo by author.*

Irish stonemason no. 317 Alexander Fegan, convicted of theft and forgery in September 1849, arrived in Fremantle on the *Mermaid* in May 1851 bearing a fourteen-year sentence. Through good conduct, he was out and about with a ticket-of-leave in December the following year. Fegan, a Catholic, married compatriot Mary Carroll (above) in York and they had at least eight children, possibly fourteen. Alexander supported his family by working as a stonemason in and around Toodyay and Albany. He died in 1903. [21] *Fremantle Prison collection.*

Coastal limestone in Fremantle varies a good deal in hardness and quality. Much that proved too soft for building was disposed of as landfill, which immediately extended The Terrace in front of the prison and provided foundations for the ramp down to the town. The Royal Engineers reported that rubbish from the town quarries was removed by horse and cart and taken to sites where it would be useful stabilising the town's sandy tracks or filling in swampy ground.

Apart from altering the topography with loads of infill, new roads and jetties, the Royal Engineers deliberately and logically proceeded with their construction of the permanent prison. Water was a priority—for thirsty labourers, for blacksmiths, to cool their heated metal, for masons, to mix their mortar—and 40 feet into the limestone a clear clean source was tapped. Eventually five wells were sunk. Water, limestone, timber and muscle were the builders' main resources.

Carpentry was a skilled craft and construction was sometimes delayed for lack of trained carpenters. Lieutenant Henry Wray reported in August 1852:

> The whole of the works have been materially delayed by the small number of Carpenters and labourers. By care and a little practice, a handy prisoner soon learns to build sufficiently well to obviate the want of masons—but of course Carpenters cannot be so easily taught.[22]

Timber, required for flooring and ceiling, for scaffolding, for formwork and for fires, was either bought locally or extracted from the forest along the Swan River by convicts who floated or carted the tree trunks to Fremantle. Depots at Freshwater Bay and Mount Eliza were established for those early timberworkers and axemen. Local

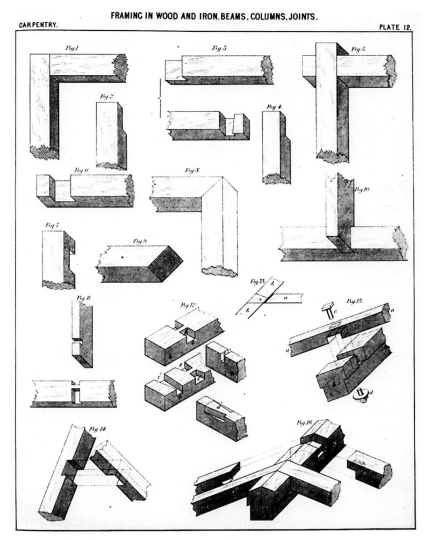

FRAMING IN WOOD AND IRON. BEAMS. COLUMNS. JOINTS.

CARPENTRY.

PLATE 12.

Joinery of the type practised in the 1860s, as shown in R. S. Burn's *The New Guide to Carpentry: general framing and joinery.*

technology was unsophisticated. The colony had only one crude sawmill and no drying kilns, so once at Fremantle the logs were cut in saw-pits or with a circular saw imported from England. Scrap pieces fuelled the lime kilns. Wray later wrote:

> The plan lately adopted in Western Australia to season it, was to leave the logs in the sea for a few weeks and then draw them up on the beach and cover them with a few inches of seaweed, taking care to prevent the sun getting at their ends. My experience led me to conclude that logs might lie in this way without injury for almost any length of time. Boards were cut seven inches wide, and stacked so as to admit a free circulation of air for five or six months before using.[23]

Jarrah excited the Royal Engineers, whose imperial vision set newly discovered building resources into a wider perspective than that provided by their colonial surroundings. They reported to their colleagues in London that this wood appeared more resistant than teak to terredo worm and termites. Samples were sent to the chemical laboratory at Woolwich, where the timber was thoroughly examined and tested. There it was found that jarrah was impregnated with a resin that deterred insect pests. Forests were to be felled later in the nineteenth century and much timber exported to pave streets and build jetties.

While the Royal Engineers' skills had to be adapted to the colonial environment and available materials, prison fittings such as iron window and door frames, hammock hooks, locks and keys and all the furnishings were imported from Britain. Every convict ship arrived laden, and all the iron fittings installed to secure the prisoners during the voyage were extracted and refashioned by the smiths.

8

PLACES, SPACES AND PRISON ROUTINE

Henderson designed three types of living space that reflected the regulated routine under which the convicts were to live. There were Association rooms on two levels at the northern and southern ends of the building where in theory, up to eighty men (in practice, no more than sixty) slept in hammocks strung on a wooden frame. Here, the probationary prisoners who were earning their right to a ticket-of-leave, were to repose in considerable discomfort, watched over by a single warder. A large and stinking wooden tub constituted all the toilet facilities to be had, and from the upstairs room it had to be carried down an external spiral staircase each morning to be emptied.

These staircases were later dismantled and the dormitories used for other purposes. To the north, a Catholic chapel was installed upstairs, and the space below became at various times a hospital, a gymnasium and a cinema. At the southern end, a library and kitchen were established.

Henderson's long block of single cells, standing four storeys high and divided by a wide internal corridor, provided the second level of accommodation. From the ground floor pavement, warders could view 587 individual cell doors. Each room was meant to be 4 feet wide, 7 feet long and with a ceiling of 8 feet—the same as in Portland Prison, the model for Fremantle. (There were also a few larger rooms

In consequence of complaints made of the effluvia arising from the urine tubs used in these wards, it was desirable, on sanitary grounds, to erect closets for the use of the men. A water closet has been attached to each of the associated wards, the supply cistern [being] in the roof of the main prison.[24]

Doorway viewed from the outside. *Photo by author.*

that could hold three or five men. They resulted from the speed with which Wray completed the building.) Within each small space the standard equipment comprised a hammock, two blankets and a sheet (when available), a stool, a table and a washbasin, complete with tap and running water. The men were also provided with a Bible and a prayer book. Every morning the inmate folded his bedding and unfastened his hammock at one end to hang neatly from one set of hooks at the other. He then was expected to clean the cleared space while waiting for his door to be unlocked.

Single cells, rather than dormitories, allowed men to be classified and treated individually. If the prisoner was undergoing a period of separate confinement in the Convict Establishment, he had to stay in his tiny cell for up to 21 hours a day. He ate, slept and worked there, being allowed out only for some exercise and to attend chapel services. The number of months of enforced solitude, supposed to turn his thoughts towards a better life, varied. Colonial prisoners sentenced to transportation, and who served time in Fremantle, passed at least three months this way, as did those convicts who reoffended with serious crimes and were returned to the Establishment. But, at the beginning of the prison's life, few in the single cells endured such strict discipline. Most joined their fellows already in the Association wards who laboured outside the prison. Others helped in daily routines. They cooked the food, supervised by the master cook or master baker (who were warders), washed the dirty clothes and swept and washed the prison itself. They were also trained in tailoring, printing, bootmaking and other skills that might come in handy as free men.

The cell walls were bare, cleanly covered with a lime wash in a vain endeavour to control insects like cockroaches that moved into the porous stone as soon as the walls were erected. These pests tormented inmates during the history of the prison, creeping over their faces at night, fouling their bedding, staining clothing and books. The cockroaches foiled all efforts to eradicate them and were still evident in 1991 when the prison closed.

Whitewash

Take a clean, water-tight barrel, or other suitable cask, and put into it half a bushel of lime. Slake it by pouring boiling water over it, boiling hot and in sufficient quantity to cover it five inches deep, and stir it briskly till thoroughly slaked. When the slaking has been effected, dissolve it in water, and add two pounds of sulphate of zinc and one of common salt; these will cause the wash to harden and prevent its cracking…[25]

The lime wash, although a failure in pest control, was more successful at revealing attempts at forbidden decoration. Prisoners were not supposed to draw on the walls, but convict number 5,569, James Walsh, who had been reconvicted for forgery in 1859, sketched paintings from memory throughout his cell. He is said to have hidden them by the clever expedient of smearing his breakfast porridge on the wall each morning—an unlikely tale, given the spare prison diet, but if true, a generous sacrifice to art. Once found, his efforts were obliterated. Ironically, the layers of wash applied for this purpose instead preserved them, and his cell drawings were rediscovered in 1964. With the paint since removed, the images can still be viewed today. Among the known works of Walsh, who died in May 1871, are two watercolour landscapes of Perth and twelve pencil and watercolour sketches of Aborigines.[26]

Other prisoners may also have written or drawn on cell walls, but it was not until the 1980s that any such painting was officially permitted. The Convict Establishment had no place for art. It was

Forger James Walsh's talents also included pencil and watercolour sketches. These drawings on his cell wall were rediscovered in 1964. *Fremantle Prison collection.*

constructed to confine and control.

Behind the main block stood the punishment cells in their own yard—the third kind of accommodation on the site. Nearby is said to have been the triangle on which men were flogged. Corporal punishment disappeared from Fremantle Prison only in 1943, when the last flogging took place. If this brutal event left scars on the victim, equally it affected observers like Dr Allan Bean, who is said to have returned from the flogging 'ghastly white and sickened, revolted by the thing he'd had to witness'. He had had to intervene, after 17 of the prescribed 25 strokes, to spare the punished man from 'serious damage'.[27]

Henderson had remonstrated with Governor Fitzgerald that a special location for ill-disciplined inmates was unnecessary given the cramped nature of the single cells. But the Governor in Perth and Jebb in London agreed that a place of secondary punishment for those who infringed prison regulations was essential. It was to be used frequently in the life of the prison. The roof of this block was sealed with concrete, contrasting with the main building's roof of slate and shingles. Each Refractory cell was furnished with two doors for extra security, a bare bed with no mattress and one or two blankets, nothing else. Until the end of the nineteenth century, six of the original eighteen cells were dark, admitting no light and little air. Apart from punishing those sentenced to solitary confinement more severely, these forbidding rooms were also used to calm men thought to be violent. Occasionally they held those described as 'lunatics'. The unfortunates sentenced to time in the dark cells were rapidly controlled, but they became disoriented and dazed because they could not tell night from day. Full daylight blinded them when they first emerged. A diet of bread and water added to the harshness of the punishment. Men were sentenced to these cells for what were declared short periods of time, usually no longer than a month, but after 1863 occasionally as long as three months. For example, on 21 September 1866 it was recorded:

> His Excellency the Governor has been pleased to direct that Reconvicted Prisoner 4800 Joseph Price be kept in a dark cell upon bread and water until the Surgeon report that he can bear it no longer and that then he be worked till further orders in the Chain Gang inside the prison.[28]

The symbolism contained in the prison design was clear. The Association rooms and the Refractory cells stood at opposite ends of the continuum of prison discipline, but were equally important in the prison plan. They represented the carrot and the stick. Between

The Refractory cells in 2004 with modern razor wire barrier in place.
Photo by author.

them stood the chapel, offering God's assistance to those caught in the system. It broke the straight, plain facade of the main cell block in the centre by jutting into the unadorned parade ground. The place of religion in the prison system and its hoped-for reformatory benefits were emphasised by its location. Optimists judged religion to be the main hope of turning convict minds towards repentance and a better life, and church services remained important in prison routine, although, as experience in British prisons had already demonstrated, Christian teaching, even when combined with the separate system, could not ensure that men did not reoffend. Jebb, as Director of Convict Prisons, accepted the argument that regular chapel attendance was important, despite the interruption it caused in the working day.

The chapel roof spanned 44 feet, supported by a laminated arch of local timbers. Lack of resources like iron and strong, burned bricks, widely used in other places to support arched structures, forced the Royal Engineers to seek another solution. Wray introduced this building technique as he completed the chapel during two years when Henderson was on leave. Positioning the first altar table was chaplain Richard Alderson's responsibility. His arrival coincided with the final stages of construction, and he no doubt also decided where the pulpit and harmonium were to be located. He had been an army chaplain, serving in the Crimea, before applying to the convict department and accepting a position in Fremantle. He stayed for twenty years, despite being robbed by his convict servants within his first two months. He married Hannah Matilda Dixon, the younger daughter of the superintendent. They had a big family of daughters, their only son dying in infancy.

Hierarchy was important in the system even in the chapel. Pews were provided for the prison officers and benches for the convicts. Brief services were held twice each day with longer ones on Sunday, when both convicts and warders were obliged to attend at least once. The superintendent occasionally recorded convict baptisms, but no font has been discovered. During the twentieth century, it is said that a bath sometimes served this purpose.

View of the chapel, attendance at which was obligatory, showing delicate wrought iron work and wall texts beyond.[29] *Fremantle Prison collection.*

Nineteenth century prisoners were supposed to belong already to one denomination or another of the Christian church. Moslems and Jews were not catered for in the convict prison world; nor at first were Catholics, apart from services performed by a local priest. Secretary of State Henry Labouchere firmly rejected any idea of building a separate chapel, although once numerous convicts arrived from Ireland it was clearly desirable. In 1862 a doorway into the upper Association ward on the northern end of the building was opened, heralding the use of this space by the Catholics. It was decorated and furnished over the years, largely with the help of donations raised from the faithful outside the walls, and it remains a consecrated space, as does the chapel.

The restored Roman Catholic chapel after the 1988 fire that swept through the northern half of the prison. *Fremantle Prison collection.*

The newly arrived prisoner would have seen the chapel after he was marched through two front gates. The first and more important entry was flanked by officers' quarters and dominated by the large chiming clock, on the upper storey of the Gatehouse. This clock in turn overlooked a courtyard bounded by the smaller, inner gateway inscribed with three names, H. Wray RE, J. Manning and Joseph Nelson. Wray apparently designed the gate, Manning, as clerk of works, supervised its construction and Nelson, a soldier with the Royal Sappers and Miners, was the blacksmith who wrought the metal. Very few architectural details within the prison buildings are named or claimed in this way. It seems likely that, even more than bridging the chapel roof, these three men saw constructing the inner iron gates as some private triumph. Wray reported their success blandly enough:

> A pair of iron gates with small side gates have been prepared and fixed at the entrance leading from the outer yard to the prison. These gates have been made principally from the iron from convict ships, which from its generally inferior quality is unfit for ordinary purposes, where welding is required. They have been so constructed as not to require welding, and, as finished, present a good appearance, and are a substantial as well as economical piece of work.[30]

Once beyond the entry complex, the prisoner was meant to feel dwarfed by the size of the cell block which dominated a wide empty space. Gardens from time to time have decorated some of this area, but Henderson did not wish to clutter the formal emptiness of this zone. He left the ground flat and plain so that the glare reflected by limestone gravel affected everyone. Clear space encircled the building in order that warders might see any attempted escape, but,

The Wray inner gates. *Fremantle Prison collection.*

in the first years of the prison, the yards at the back were full of holes and quarry shafts. Discipline was not always as rigorous as official reports claimed. Ladders were dropped around the place, piles of rock stood beside the walls, and, as a consequence, some notable escapes took place. Moondyne Joe, a known escaper, assiduously piled rocks he was meant to be breaking into gravel beside the front wall, cast his jacket over two picks stuck in the ground with a hat perched on top, and shinned up and into the yard of one of the front houses. Luckily for him a gate was open, and he was off into the bush. Other men flung ladders against the wall, but were inevitably caught. One man climbed through the roof of the prison at night to shin down the lightning conductor and climb the perimeter wall. He too was returned to prison. Police, Pensioner Guards and Aboriginal trackers hunted the absconders, all of whom were eventually captured.

A kitchen, a bakehouse and washhouse, a bathhouse and a hospital were built more or less at the same time as the main block. Each employed different prison warders to oversee its function, and each had a series of prisoners employed there. The bakehouse marked the dependence the prisoners had on their bread ration, a situation which continued well into the twentieth century. Convicts ate it with each meal. It was prepared in 8- and 10-ounce loaves each

Bread was still important in the twentieth century prison diet. *Fremantle Prison collection.*

day, then stored for 24 hours because doctors believed new bread was difficult to digest. Breakfast was usually bread and black tea; the evening meal was bread and tea or cocoa.

The recipe for bread used in the prison bakery included quantities of potato-based yeast. In October 1850 the yeast required 24 lb of malt, 4 lb of hops and 64 lb of potatoes. No doubt the directions varied with the number of men in the prison and the availability of the ingredients.

Lunch (then called dinner) was the main meal. Soup was served, followed by meat and vegetables. The meat was steamed in large boilers brought from England, a modern cooking technique for the times, and potatoes, rice or oatmeal were boiled. In 1876 the meanness of prison life became apparent to a new superintendent, who discovered that inmates were reduced to eating their solid food from the same towel they wiped themselves with after work, as they required their one tin plate for their soup. He was appalled and requisitioned more plates immediately.

Fifty years later, when the prison was inspected by members of the Women's Service Guild, the kitchen seemed to be equipped with the same cooking apparatus still turning out the same meals.

Huge copper boilers contain the hominy, soup, meat and potatoes. Steam is used for heating these coppers...In the bakehouse...prisoners were moulding, weighing and placing the long eight ounce and ten ounce loaves on trays for the oven.[31]

The convict was fed three times a day, his clothes were washed once a week, and he was permitted one bath a week, sometimes more in summer. (Even in the 1970s inmates were permitted to shower only three times a week.) These simple matters, which we now take

Cooking equipment in the prison kitchen. *Fremantle Prison collection.*

Laundry, like all other prison routines, was regulated. *Fremantle Prison collection.*

for granted, resulted from a careful scrutiny of diet in institutions and from the more formal prison regimes initiated in the nineteenth century. Convict clothes were either made in Fremantle from fabric brought in from England, or were tailored in English prisons. Dixon was often dissatisfied with the appearance of the convicts, claiming that their clothing was ill-suited to local conditions. The broad arrow, or an identifying stripe of colour in the material, marked convict clothes and bedding.

Personal cleanliness was emphasised. The washbasin in each cell was meant to be used, but not as a urinal, its most common fate. Yet a hot bath was a luxury, as it was for most people, and the convicts suffered badly from skin complaints. The bathhouse had a hand pump to bring water to the surface to fill the twenty-five lead-lined concrete baths, and a boiler, which was stoked by prisoners, but only in the winter months. During the summer, bath water was cold. The waste fed into the main drains beneath the cell block in the belief that it would wash away all smells that had accumulated there from the cell basins and water closets. It was then to be 'deodorised' by a charcoal filter and theoretically could be drawn on to irrigate the prison garden before dropping into two large cesspits, one on each side of the entry ramp. Unhappily for the inmates, this idea was unsuccessful. The drains were too large in diameter and had too short a fall for the waste or the smells to dissipate. The main cell block quickly acquired a persistent stench, especially on the ground floor. Individual cell furnishings of wash basin and tap, luxury fittings of the day that might have been envied by most Perth householders, were in fact an expensive disaster constantly in need of attention. They were eventually removed.

As the Superintendent wrote to the Comptroller General in January 1863:

I have the honour to inform you that the Surgeon has called
my attention to the necessity of remedying the very foul smell
which issues through the plug holes in the bottom of some of
the basins in the cellular division proceeding from the sewer
through the waste water pipes.

I have long been aware of the existence of this evil both
from personal observation and from the Report of the Principal
Warder in charge of the Division but not seeing how it could
be remedied I have heretofore refrained from reporting it
officially.

The fact I ascribe principally to two causes namely 1st that
the plugs belonging to the basins are in many cases obliged
to be left unfixed in their proper positions to permit the water
which constantly drops from the taps to run off, since in many
cases the leakage through the taps is so great that it will fill a
basin and hence overflow in the course of two or three hours.

2ndly The wooden bank drain under the prison wall which
receives the waste water from these pipes is of much too small
a section and is laid too horizontally so as soon to get choked
with a deposit of filth from which of course a noxious odour
exhales.[32]

Plumbing was also defective in English prisons, and water-closets
installed with care and expense in Pentonville were to be removed
at much the same time as the basins in Fremantle. In both prisons
convicts had used the fixtures to hide illicit goods, like knives or
crudely made guns, and in Pentonville the pipes had become a
means of communication, which subverted the entire purpose of
separate confinement.

The prison surgeon, George Cook Attfield, whose opinions on

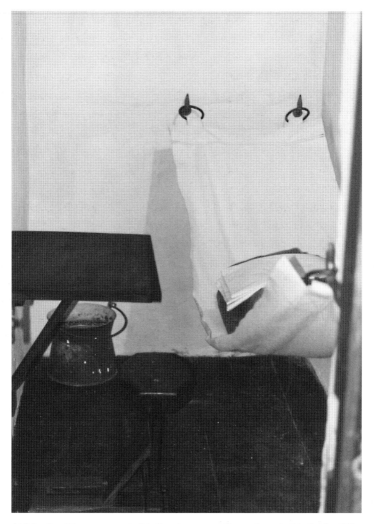

With plumbing removed, this is what a convict cell probably looked like in the 1870s. The cell was restored and furnished in the 1990s. *Fremantle Prison collection.*

Fremantle's basins were ultimately to cause their removal, ran the hospital assisted by convict wardsmen. The building itself stands behind the cell block, backing on to the eastern boundary wall in order to catch the best summer breezes and the maximum winter sunlight. Since 1908 another building, New Division, has blocked its view, but it is still possible to see how isolated the hospital once was from the main prison structure. Here came men who had ophthalmia, a common colonial complaint, tuberculosis, an incurable illness that the prison doctors noted sometimes receded in Western Australia, and various gastric and skin diseases. And here they received treatment at least as expert as any they might have received outside the prison.

The surgeon's pharmacopoeia was replenished from London and included herbs and palliatives, as well as compounds of mercury and other minerals, splints and bandages. His medical journals and registers, where he noted the illnesses and the treatments administered, show the limitations of what he had available to ease pain or to cure serious complaints. Those unfortunate few who were injured as they quarried stone, or who fell from scaffolding while building, were immediately attended to, but without antibiotics or modern pain-relieving drugs. In 1870 the superintendent recorded the kind of accident which he deemed 'as one of a class which no practicable care will entirely or effectually prevent'. Two men had been working as members of the bridge quarry party, and

> had drilled four holes for blasting, they had loaded and tamped three of these holes or drills, and had loaded the fourth hole and were in the act of tamping it when it exploded, and both these men were blown from it.[33]

One was severely injured, the other less so; the supervising warder, he carefully noted, was not to be blamed.

Attfield attended to the health of the prisoners for twenty years. His responsibilities included care of mentally ill convicts, as well as the warders and their families. Insane convicts were not treated in the prison hospital. Their cries upset the sane. Once the permanent prison was complete, convict (and free) lunatics were confined in the Scott buildings where the colony's first padded cell was installed. The continuing request from the medical men during the 1850s for a lunatic asylum came to fruition in the 1860s, when the Fremantle Lunatic Asylum was built by convicts, providing a much-needed facility to be used by both bond and free, men and women. It has been preserved as the Fremantle Arts Centre.

Surgeon Attfield wrote in 1870 that an exceptionally large number of inmates were under observation, seventeen of whom were ultimately sent to the asylum.

I think it is universally admitted that, combined with the low uncultivated intellect and the life of dissipation and excitement led by the majority of prisoners previous to incarceration, prison discipline generally, by its monotony, its periods of separate confinement and its other various causes of depression always tends, more or less, to develop any proclivity to insanity. I think further also that this country, by its excessive heat at times, its sterile uninteresting prospect and by its dearth of sources of amusement intellectual or physical, is peculiarly favourable to the manifestation of any lurking or latent predisposition to insanity, but, as stated before, I do not think that the discipline or other influences specially attaching to this Prison can be adduced as unduly tending to this result.[34]

Lunatic Asylum while it was being restored to become the Fremantle Arts Centre.
Fremantle City Library Local History collection, No. 769.

Also preserved is Edmund Henderson's magnificent home, The Knowle, which he designed and completed using convict labour by the end of 1852. Today it is almost hidden behind the additions of Fremantle Hospital. From its wide verandas he could watch warders walking to their shift, parties of convicts emerging for their day's labour, and he could hear the prison clock chime. He wrote to his father that Governor Fitzgerald was very appreciative of his beautiful home, which he had decorated with red flock wallpaper and a splendid chandelier. Indeed, after Henderson returned to London, the then colonial governor, Sir John Hampton, did his best to acquire it. He was denied the pleasure because it was owned by the British

Government, as were all the Convict Establishment buildings.

It was at The Knowle that Henderson's first wife, Mary, died at the end of 1855. Her death was unexpected, although from hints Henderson had dropped in his letters it appears that she may have been in poor health. Henderson was devoted to her and so shocked at her death that he took immediate leave from his position to return to England with their son Douglas. His place was taken by Henry Wray, who was also bereaved, as he and his wife had just lost their infant son. The Wrays paid heavily for their time in Fremantle; a 15-month-old daughter, Alice, had previously died on the voyage out. They buried their boy in the new Protestant cemetery (now the playing fields of John Curtin Senior High School) near the memorial they had erected for Alice. The wife of the Comptroller General lay there too, far from the family home she never saw again once she

The Knowle as it appeared last century. *Fremantle Prison collection.*

left Canada, such was the harsh fate of army wives. Henderson did not return to Fremantle until 1858, when he brought his second wife, Maria Augusta Walcott, to The Knowle. She bore him four daughters during the four years they lived there, and another two in England. As can be seen from their letters to each other, this second marriage was also happy. The couple died within weeks of each other in 1896.

The variety of housing and the prison, together with the barracks, their parade grounds and the commissariat, transformed the small village of Fremantle into a town. It was a prison, police and military town, its buildings largely owned by the British Government. The architecture displayed for all to see who was who in the Convict Establishment.

9

THEORIES BEHIND TRANSPORTATION

Fremantle's Convict Establishment was part of the British convict prison system, and understandably the prison's design, discipline and routines were affected by debates taking place in London. Prison reform had been brought to the attention of many thoughtful people by John Howard, whose book comparing prisons at home and abroad, published before the First Fleet landed at Botany Bay, emphasised the desperate conditions suffered by inmates.[35]

By the mid-nineteenth century convict prisons were undergoing radical transformation from being holes in the ground and places of disintegration, despair and death. They had evolved into institutions where a man could expect to be regularly fed, clothed and educated, albeit with every detail of his sentence and behaviour recorded and assessed. Transportation also changed from the dire punishment described by historians of the First and Second Fleets, to a more measured response—not only to crime but also to the colony that received the convicts. Men sent to Western Australia were told they had the opportunity of becoming useful colonists, if they amended their ways.

Writing in 1777, the inspirational Howard had described convicts as:

...generally stout robust young men, who have been accustomed to free diet, tolerable lodgings, and vigorous exercise. These are ironed, and thrust into close offensive dungeons, and there chained down, some of them, without straw or other bedding; in which they continue, in winter, sixteen or seventeen hours out of the twenty-four, in utter inactivity, and immersed in the noxious effluvia of their own bodies. On this account, the gaol-distemper is always observed to reign more in our prisons during winter than summer; contrary, I presume, to the nature of other putrid diseases. Their diet is at the same time low and scanty; they are generally without firing; and the powers of life soon become incapable of resisting so many causes of sickness and despair.[36]

Measures to humanise the otherwise daunting prison environment included gardens that were planted before the First World War. *Fremantle Prison collection.*

Across society, men and women talked and argued about prison reform. Their politics, religion or philosophy may have differed, but their debates shaped the future of transportation to Fremantle. Reformers deplored crowded cells, poor food, overuse of flogging or chaining, and expected the state to remedy these matters. They did not win all the arguments. Their opponents saw merit in making prison a fearful experience, believing pain and horror would deter potential criminals. Cost was never a fully resolved issue, although the Home Office built several new prisons during the nineteenth century. Echoes of this debate can be heard today.

10

WHO WERE THE CONVICTS?

Convicts were numbered rather than named. They forfeited their identity in prison, whether as sons, brothers, father or husbands. From this personal vacuum, little correspondence has survived for their descendants to ponder.

'Convict No. 1', Samuel Scattergood, born in 1812, a gardener by occupation, unmarried and semi-literate, was an example of the kind of man the colonists thought they wanted. He received fifteen years for stealing a sheep and a term in Wakefield Prison, including thirteen months in separate confinement. That is probably where he learned to read and write, however inadequately. His conduct was described as good and his character as very good, so he fitted the description of the kind of convict the colonists demanded. He arrived on the *Scindian* in June 1850. Twelve months later he had his ticket-of-leave and was working. In 1854 he received his conditional pardon. He died in 1862.

Convicts generally were not men of high reputation or education, and the fear that they struck into many hearts is typified by novelist Charles Dickens, describing through the eyes of a child the escaped convict Magwitch in *Great Expectations*:

A fearful man, all in coarse grey, with a great iron on his leg. A man with no hat, and with broken shoes, and with an old rag tied around his head. A man who had been soaked in water, and smothered in mud, and lamed by stones, and cut by flints, and stung by nettles, and torn by briars; who limped, and shivered, and glared and growled; and whose teeth chattered in his head as he seized me by the chin.

But in Western Australia they were meant also to become colonists, somehow to emerge from the prison experience with wiser heads and a greater capacity for sustained labour than when they had entered it.

In 1857 Superintendent Dixon wrote disarmingly:

The political object of transportation is colonisation. It professes to people a remote territory by removing thither certain offenders, who, having violated the laws at home, are therefore assumed, for the future, to be dangerous members of the community. By removing such offenders, tranquillity and order are promoted in the mother country, while the distant part of the world to which they are sent, is also benefited by their reception as colonists, who, although of evil influence in the country from which they come, may yet, under certain circumstances, be eligible in the land of their compulsory adoption, for the purposes of civilisation.[37]

During 1853, when 1,132 convicts disembarked in Fremantle (the greatest number to arrive in any one year), a new sentence of penal servitude was introduced in Great Britain. Convicts were now to spend all their time in British prisons, with no prospect of remission for good behaviour. They were not transported because their sentences were generally shorter than seven years. Henderson

Former convicts Tim the Dealer, Paddy Paternoster and Jimmy outside Castle Hotel in York, 1898. *Fremantle Prison collection.*

quickly suspended all work on the new prison, seeking reassurance that transportation would continue, which he got. In 1857 the sentence of transportation was removed from the statutes, but convicts continued to arrive. Four years later transportation was again challenged, and in 1863 the colony was informed that it would end within the next few years. It was nearly five years after that warning when the last transport ship, the *Hougoumont*, disembarked its human cargo in January 1868.

Was the main purpose of the Convict Establishment to punish, to reform, or to provide new settlers? Clearly the debates about transportation and the effects of punishment influenced the building of Fremantle Prison as much as the need to satisfy the colonists who wanted a cheap labour force and government investment. But reasons given for this system of exile altered over the years. As with most historical questions, the answers depended on the time they were asked and the people who thought about them. Crime and punishment remained a political issue in London during the 1860s, despite a falling crime rate. Prison administrators admitted to a growing difficulty in finding men to transport. After 1857 most new offenders were sentenced to four years penal servitude (a sentence which had no provision for release on ticket-of-leave), rather than the previous seven years transportation. To satisfy Western Australian demand, the Bermuda convict station was closed and its inmates redirected to Fremantle. Between 1861 and 1868 men with many years to serve in English prisons were sent to Western Australia. They may have been more violent and older than those sent earlier. Certainly some offenders perceived as more difficult and dangerous were transported in these years. Ringleaders of riots that took place in Chatham Prison in 1861 were swiftly despatched to Fremantle. So were sixty-two Fenians, six of whom were to escape to the United States on the *Catalpa* in 1876. They arrived on the last ship, the *Hougoumont*. These decisions did not please the colonial elite, but they did suit the home government.

11

THE ROYAL ENGINEERS'
UNDERSTANDING

In March 1861 Henderson wrote glowingly of the prison, 'As regards every facility for the enforcement of order, cleanliness, and regularity, there is nothing to be desired, and this prison will bear comparison with any in these respects'.[38] In 1863 he told a Royal Commission that 'the success of the system has been something extraordinary. The peace and the quiet which prevails in the colony is something which nobody would believe who did not go there.'[39]

In January 1863 the Royal Engineers' office produced a score card of the benefits so far delivered to the colony by convict labour. The following selection from their record does not include buildings. In just over twelve years convicts had cleared 563 miles of road; made and repaired 563 miles of road; drained 167 miles of road; and paved four miles with pitcher paving and one mile with wooden blocks. They had constructed 6,600 yards of stone causeway and $7\frac{1}{2}$ miles of earth embankment; erected or extensively repaired 239 bridges; built 12,900 yards of bridge approaches; procured and stacked 158,300 yards of stone; broken up 65,800 yards of stone for macadamising; dug and screened 54,000 yards of gravel; felled 4,000 trees and removed them from roads; made and repaired 543 culverts; sunk 44 wells; laid and repaired $14\frac{1}{2}$ miles of tramway; cut into scantling 2,650 loads of mahogany timber; and prepared and erected 2,260 yards of fencing. They had also built two jetties and a sea wall 280 feet long which supported the roadway in Fremantle's south bay.

Add to this infrastructure significant buildings such as the North Fremantle traffic bridge, two lighthouses in Albany, Government House and the Town Hall in Perth, a residence for the governor on Rottnest, plus various precincts in country centres, Pensioner Guards cottages and the prison, and it appears beyond doubt that convict labour contributed to the colonial domain.

Henderson's perception of his time in Fremantle was professional. He retired in 1862 believing that a civilian could now be employed as Comptroller General at a reduced cost to Treasury. Management of public works had passed largely, although not completely, to the colonial government (James Manning was now in charge of them) and he could see that transportation was winding down. The comment of the clerk in the Colonial Office on Henderson's letter of resignation is revealing: 'His object is, I suppose a Colonial government'.[40] After enjoying farewell dinners, and accepting the gratitude of settlers relieved not to have been murdered or robbed, thanks, in their view, to his control of the convicts, Henderson and his family sailed home to England via Madras. There, another Royal Engineer, Sir William Denison, who had been one of his officers in England, had become Governor, having transferred from his position as Governor General in New South Wales in 1861. Henderson arrived in London in time to attend the 1863 Royal Commission inquiring into the management and discipline within the penal system. His evidence was optimistic. He thought transportation could continue to Western Australia indefinitely since the colony was thriving and, as he had previously noted, the country was 'one vast gaol'. But men also had the 'prospect of getting an honest living' because they were removed from their old haunts and bad companions. However, Henderson's view was now out of date. The discipline applied in Fremantle was a bit too liberal for the commissioners. Punishment and deterrence were to be emphasised more.

12

PUNISHMENTS AND ESCAPES

After 1863 conditions in all convict prisons became increasingly spartan and punishments more severe. In Fremantle the public soon became aware that not all convicts were promising young men eager to be reformed by the penal system. Men who reoffended within the colony were punished with time in chain gangs. They clanked along Fremantle's streets on their way to a quarry or to the river, where they were employed dredging channels or building a bridge.

Mrs Millett recorded her first impression of a chain gang encountered on the streets of Fremantle in the 1860s:

> Confirmed runaways, who had given much trouble to the police, were punished by being placed in the chain-gang at the 'Establishment'; but there were some men who seemed to be proof against all impediments, and more than one escape, even from this heavily-ironed crew occurred whilst we were in the colony. The fetters that they carried were of such size and weight that the first time I ever saw the gang I turned my head on its approach to look, as I supposed, at a jingling team of horses coming up behind us. I then perceived that the noise was caused by the irons on the legs and feet of fifty men who were walking, or rather shuffling along, in ranks of four abreast, and dressed in parti-coloured clothes. Before the prisoners marched soldiers

with mounted bayonets, and behind, bringing up the rear, were other soldiers carrying revolvers on the full cock.[41]

Another consequence of the new regime appeared to be an increase in attempts to escape. Men made rope ladders from their sheets and threw them over the walls, they scraped holes in their cell walls to hide weapons or, more regularly, just walked away from work parties outside the walls. Moondyne Joe, whose real name was Joseph Bolitho Johns, became notorious for escaping and evading capture. He had been transported for ten years for stealing food. In the colony he stole horses and lived on his own in the bush. But he acquired popular fame when he was apprehended in his last attempt at freedom while siphoning wine from the cellar of an eminent Swan Valley vigneron—an act even honest citizens probably envied. Doggerel published after his escape in 1867, sung to the tune of 'Pop goes the Weasel', was directed at Governor John Hampton and his unpopular son, the Acting Comptroller General.

> *The Governor's son has got the pip,*
> *The Governor's got the measles*
> *But Moondyne Joe has give 'em the slip.*
> *Pop goes the weasel.*

In May 1864 eight escapees had been in solitary confinement in the Refractory cells for fifty days and the surgeon requested their release. Escapes and absconding continued throughout the life of the prison; the last recorded attempt took place in 1989.

Moondyne Joe was not a violent man, nor was another inveterate escaper, Joseph Ralph. He had been convicted of burglary at the Lincoln Assizes and, because of his record, was transported for twenty years, arriving at Fremantle in 1854 aged 35. Ralph was mild-mannered and

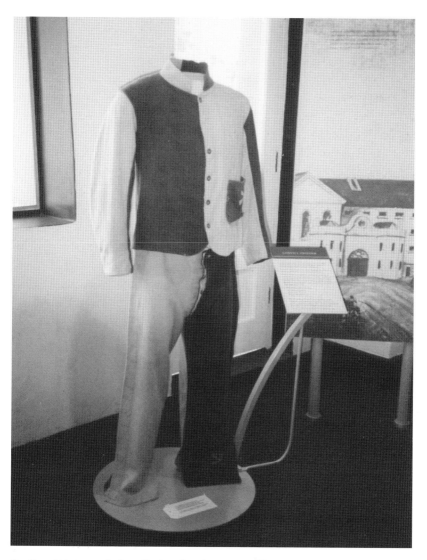

Replica chain gang clothes displayed in the prison. *Photo by author.*

became a favourite of Richard Alderson, the chaplain. He was found work in the prison library (often a haven for less robust prisoners), and recommended for his release on a ticket-of-leave in 1861. He was soon back, sentenced to two terms of three years hard labour. The chaplain wrote that he was sure of Ralph's sincerity, just as long as he was not tempted by bad companions. But he was a 'clever burglar, brought up to it as it were, and when assailed by tempters, his own fancied strength proved real weakness'. Alderson also noted critically that Ralph was lazy, and 'of all men there is least hope of the reformation of an idle man'.[42] Prison became his only world, although he attempted to escape its clutches on several occasions.

In 1864 he endured six months solitary confinement as the result of one attempt. Ten years later he was still anxious to leave. The superintendent found 'sundry prohibited articles and false keys' in his cell. He was ordered before the visiting magistrate and sentenced to time in the Refractory cells. Treatment of Ralph illustrated the prison administrators' sensibilities when, after being flogged and spending time in solitary confinement, he was secured in a cell reinforced with timber battens and clout nails, and said to be 'the most secure cell in this Prison'. He was also strip-searched twice daily.

There were three such places in the prison, one now called Moondyne Joe's cell, but it might equally have been Ralph's. Men like these tended to be loners, angry at their perceived injustices and with a horror of all that prison discipline could do. But they could not evade the power of the system. Johns, after a long life, died in the Lunatic Asylum in 1900; Ralph expired in the prison hospital in 1887.

Consistency, which is believed to be a crucial element in the application of penal ideologies, was rarely achieved. It was undermined both within and without the prison by changing circumstances. In October 1866, while 'escape mania' was affecting

Moondyne Joe. *Fremantle Prison collection and Ian Elliot.*

the inmates, the iron class, or chain gang, finished building the North Fremantle traffic bridge. The clerk of works, James Manning, was pleased at the completion of this substantial structure and—proud of his creation and his workforce—asked the Governor to mark the occasion with an official opening. Hampton, a stickler for consistency, declined to honour the convicts. So Manning arranged to open the bridge with an unofficial ceremony. On 26 October the Fremantle Volunteers made a moonlight march from their parade ground below the prison to the traffic bridge. They were joined by a rag-tag crowd of locals who cheered them on. They proceeded to the centre of the span where, it was reported:

> [they] halted, fixed bayonets, took open order and presented arms, whilst the Band played 'God Save the Queen'; after which they resumed close order, unfixed bayonets and lodged arms, and the band played a few tunes.[43]

They moved to the north side, then returned to the centre to hear the national anthem once more and give three cheers for Governor Hampton, perhaps ironically offered since the Governor was visiting Champion Bay, many miles north of Perth, before marching back to their parade ground. Manning also arranged for his gang of convicts to be rewarded with extra rations, acknowledging that they were men as well as prisoners.

Penal routines never completely banished personal initiative. Men sentenced to hard labour dredged the mouth of the Swan River—a poor excuse for a harbour pending the arrival in the 1890s of engineer C. Y. O'Connor, who succeeded in removing the obstructing rock and sandbars without the use of prisoners. Back in 1869, when escapees were still making news, the Duke of Edinburgh

James Manning's impressive achievement was widely applauded, but to irreverent wags it was the 'Bridge of Styx'. *Fremantle City Library Local History collection, No. 350.*

(Queen Victoria's second oldest son) graced one of the Empire's more distant colonies with a royal visit. His trip to the antipodes was studded with incident, including an assassination attempt made on his life in Sydney by a Fenian. In Fremantle, after a ceremonial greeting by the Governor and dignitaries, he boarded his Perth-bound carriage just as a gun was fired, causing the horses to bolt. An accident was avoided only when a bugler had the presence of mind to 'sound the halt', which the horses fortunately obeyed. On the return trip, the Prince prudently opted for a barge trip to the port, rather than risk horses again. Unhappily, the tide was low and the vessel struck one of the many sandbanks in the Fremantle channel. A gang of convicts respectfully leapt into the water and deferentially heaved the boat over the obstruction, thus earning themselves each a year off their sentences of gang labour. The *Perth Gazette* solemnly concluded its report: 'Let us thank Providence that the Prince has left our felon-stained shores, without having had his jewelry stolen, his person mobbed, or his body the mark for an assassin's bullet'.[44]

Duke of Edinburgh. *Illustrated Sydney News, 16 September 1867, Mitchell Library, State Library of NSW (NA 108).*

13

THE BEGINNING OF THE END

In 1877 Sir Edmund Du Cane, who had claimed in 1863 that Fremantle's Convict Establishment was 'just as perfect as an English prison', was now in charge of the entire penal system. He separated colonial and imperial responsibilities for convicts and former convicts more clearly, and began to apply strict financial restrictions on the Fremantle outpost. Wages were frozen or cut, and Alderson and Attfield, who had shared a house as the prison was being completed, and had lived and worked there for twenty years, both resigned. Alderson took his daughters to Pinjarra where they established an orchard. Attfield, who in 1863 had married Alice Maude Roe, youngest daughter of the Surveyor General, returned to England with his family.

By the second half of the 1870s the inmate population was falling. The men were generally older and more hardened to prison life. To the town's continued benefit, they broke rocks in the prison yards for roads, or turned the water pump as a punishment. The Commissioner of Works, Malcolm Fraser, told the colonial Legislative Council in December 1875 that

a tank is being constructed by convict labour within the Establishment grounds. This tank which is of brick lined with cement, has been estimated to hold about 67,000 gallons of water and will be filled during winter from the rainfall off the roofs of the main building, and the supply kept up during the dry season from wells by means of pumps...[45]

The water was delivered to Long Jetty where ships paid sixpence for 100 gallons. It was Fremantle's first town water supply.

By 1883 there were fewer than ninety men confined and twenty-three of them were classified as 'colonial' prisoners. Du Cane was keen to turn the prison and all its supporting buildings over to the colony, but the local legislature proved reluctant to take charge of the establishment because expensive repairs were required for which the home government adamantly refused to pay. A hard bargain was

Women warders photographed not long after Federation. *Fremantle Prison collection.*

pushed and various changes were put in place to make the prison a more viable proposition. In 1886 Perth Prison was closed and its inmates removed to Fremantle. Two years later women prisoners were accommodated on the site for the first time, in cells 7 feet by 4 feet, built within the old bakery and kitchen, behind a long wall. A new kitchen for the men was installed in a former Association room.

Invalid ex-convicts, who had lived in relative comfort in the Comptroller General's house, were resettled in the old prison hospital, leaving The Knowle to be extended in the 1890s as Fremantle's first public hospital. The prison hospital now houses the Fremantle Children's Literature Centre. Then the population began

Part of the extensive system of tunnels and drives. *Fremantle Prison collection.*

to increase and the cells began to fill. The colony was experiencing a goldrush that brought thousands of adventurers from interstate and overseas to try their luck. Not all were fortunate, but gold discoveries transformed Western Australia from a modest backwater to a more flourishing place. New wealth and a forward-looking government fostered a building boom. Fremantle harbour finally became a reality, and trade in wheat and other primary products began to transform the port into a city. Inside the prison, which was now overcrowded, inmates excavated under the walls, not to escape but in pursuit of another water supply for the growing town.

Brick entry to water reservoir, built in 1890s. *Photo by author.*

14

CAPITAL PUNISHMENT

Under colonial management a gallows was constructed near the Refractory cells, all death sentences previously having been carried out in Perth Prison. The first man executed, in 1889, was Long Jimmy, alias Jimmy Long, a murderer from Penang. The first nine men condemned to death in Fremantle were Asian, illustrating perhaps the difficult working conditions of indentured labourers in the north-west. The last execution was that of serial killer Eric Cooke in 1964. The only woman hanged at Fremantle was Martha Rendell, executed in 1909 for causing the death of one of her stepchildren, an accusation she always denied. Hers was a sad story that did not convince those who judged her. She was a married woman who had left her husband to live with another's and look after his children. They moved to East Perth, a poor area of the town where noxious trades like tanneries poured filth into the river. Claisebrook drain was a health hazard. Three of the children became ill with sore throats, possibly diphtheria, a dreaded childhood illness, and died. She was alleged to have painted their throats with a poison that hastened their deaths. Her case received a lot of publicity and divided Perth's population. There were those who thought no woman should be hanged, and those who believed all murderers must be executed. Some could not accept she was guilty. Petitions were signed and letters written to the Press—all to no avail.

Prisoners sentenced to death were removed from the main prison population to the condemned cell where they were observed night and day by prison officers who recorded every move they made, every morsel they ate. Because of the attempts made on Martha Rendell's behalf for clemency, she remained for three weeks in this situation. On the morning of her execution the sheriff's deputy, the executioner, chaplain, medical officer, superintendent and two female officers escorted her to the gallows. The executioner was not usually a warder. He was an independent contract worker paid for each job. As with flogging, it proved difficult to find a local person to accept the position, and during the twentieth century the executioner was brought in from the eastern states. At 8 am an unusually crowded gallery of twenty-five witnesses gathered in the small chamber, including principal warders and other officers. The white cap was adjusted on the condemned woman's head, the rope was placed around her neck and the trapdoor released. If the executioner had done his work properly, death would have taken place immediately. According to Press accounts, culled from observers since reporters were not present, Martha Rendell was pronounced dead by three minutes past the hour.[46]

These formal proceedings could upset observers, and it was not unknown for officers to faint. On the day that an execution took place, the prison atmosphere might be charged with fear and other emotions, particularly if inmates had known the condemned person. The death penalty was removed from the statute books in 1984 after 44 people had been hanged in Fremantle Prison.

EPILOGUE

Prisons have often sent us ambiguous messages. Although the Convict Establishment was modern in its day, and the Royal Engineers brought many good ideas to the colony, transportation was an old method of punishment and ultimately a flawed way of colonising the western third of the continent. Judgments of the convict system may vary, but it was always responsible for dislocation and pain. Families today may be happy to reclaim a convict ancestor, but during the nineteenth century it was another story. People then kept quiet about the shame of having a convict relative. Some men made successful transitions into colonial life; many did not. Plenty left for other parts of the country and other parts of the world. No doubt a few returned to England to reclaim their personal history. Western Australia was a foreign country for them, yet, under the discipline and prison routine, the convicts constructed a series of buildings, especially in Fremantle, which created a new landscape and gave impetus to a new colonial confidence. The rush of new settlers, and the input of merchants, shipping companies, banks and wharf labourers that followed the gold discoveries, transformed the town, building around and over the older structures, often burying their significance.

Imprisonment also changed. Executions took place within the gaol, instead of in public view. There was no longer a perceived need to terrify the public with the implementation of the law. The sight of someone slowly being strangled, dangling from a noose, was deemed a private affair. Chain gangs too retreated from the streets and prison labour was to be devalued during the twentieth century. Trade unions mounted campaigns against its use, seeking to protect their members against the competition of poorly remunerated workers. The prison slowly became a closed world accountable only to those who forced explanations from its administrators.

As a result of one campaign for change in 1899, the colonial parliament convened an inquiry into Fremantle Prison. Commissioners discovered that inmates were still living under convict rules and regulations: chains, floggings, dark cells and bread and water rations remained in use. They thought it all out of date and recommended several innovations, among them electricity, better plumbing and a new building. The parliamentarians studied theories of punishment and came to the conclusion that segregation was worth another try. The main cell block was divided into four, allowing inmates to be classified and removed from each other according to their sentence. 'Separate' imprisonment was briefly imposed again in New Division, but the world had moved on. It was no longer feasible to expect that silence and solitary musings would improve a confined man's disposition. During the twentieth century further new policies were instituted, tested and discarded in their turn. There is no such thing as a 'perfect prison'.

In the 1920s it was belatedly realised that, under the Health Act, Henderson's cells were too small. 'Common boarding houses' were obliged to provide greater space and more air per person than was possible in Fremantle Prison. Portland Prison, Henderson's model, where the walls had been sheets of galvanised iron, could be, and was, readily altered. It was a bit more difficult in Fremantle where the limestone walls represented a challenge. Not all the cells were doubled in size. A few originals have been maintained and in recent years some have been restored. They are part of a program to illustrate changes that took place as the result of continuing concern with crime, punishment, reform and the frequent failure to prevent reoffending.

Change is a continuing story in Fremantle. Today, as we walk through the city, savouring the aroma of good coffee along the capuccino strip, or appreciating the pleasures offered by the restored west end buildings, we can only see the convict past if we look closely. From the Roundhouse our view down High Street takes us to the Town Hall, completed in 1887, and eastwards to the grim prison walls. Their impact is softened now by nearby housing, trees, carparks and a football field. We glance south to the Fishing Boat Harbour, refurbished in time for the America's Cup in 1986-87 and see also the Maritime Museum Shipwrecks Gallery and the Norfolk Island pines firmly established in reclaimed land. To the north-east lies the John Curtin Senior High School; lying before it is the old Lunatic Asylum, now Fremantle's Art Centre and History Museum. The bones of this landscape were set by convict workers whose labour turned a fishing village into a town with a future.

Fremantle Prison was emptied of inmates in 1991. Now it is a heritage site that teaches us how ideas about prisons and confinement developed over time. Free men and women walk though its corridors and cells. Our society has largely shed its colonial fears, replacing them with others. We are more likely to worry about international terrorism and its proper punishment, or to debate issues of nationality, race and racism, and environmental problems, than to work for prison reform, even though greater numbers are crowding Australian prisons than ever before. We still suffer from crime; we still seek retribution for criminal activity; a few still think longingly of capital punishment. But we often leave these matters to be discussed superficially, if at all. Yet we have moved a good distance from exiling felons to another country, and from the history of hanging a shivering teenager on a rock overlooking an alien ocean.

NOTES

Abbreviations used in Notes and Further reading
CUP Cambridge University Press
MUP Melbourne University Press
OUP Oxford University Press
UWAP University of Western Australia Press

[1] Cited in I. Berryman (ed.), *Swan River Letters*, Perth 2002. vol. 1, p. 267.
[2] G. Bolton et al (eds), *The Wollaston Journals,* UWAP, Nedlands, 1991–92, vol. 2, p. 28.
[3] 'Report on the Convict Establishment', *The Independent Journal*, 5 July 1850.
[4] All records of prison routine come from the Convict Prison Records, State Records Office, Acc. 1156; see also Further reading. Comptroller General's correspondence with the Colonial Secretary in Perth, 1850 and 1851, details these punishments.
[5] 'Fremantle Esplanade' files deposited by Fremantle City Council in State Records Office give a full description of the park's development.
[6] 'Convict Store Accounts 1854 to 1860' in Convict Prison Records, State Records Office, lists goods carried by the *Lord Raglan.*
[7] Henderson's report in 1851 can be found in his second half-yearly report, Convict Prison Records, now on microfilm in the Battye Library. Reports of this nature from various Australian penal colonies were tabled in the House of Commons, later to be published as parliamentary papers entitled *Australian Colonies. Convict Discipline and Transportation. Further Correspondence.*
[8] The Superintendent's Letterbooks and official convict prison correspondence provide lists of clothing and equipment issued to ticket-of-leave men.
[9] Superintendent Dixon's correspondence with Comptroller General, 1854–55.
[10] See Fremantle Prison collection for further information on clocks gathered by the archivist.
[11] Useful biographical information on persons mentioned in this book can be found in the *Dictionary of Western Australians* (see Further reading).

[12] Superintendent's Letterbook, 1861–63.

[13] Superintendent Lefroy to Comptroller General, correspondence 1862. Rules for running the prison were worked out between these two officials, using guidelines from British convict prisons, especially from Portland Prison.

[14] Details from the file 'F. J. Townsend', Fremantle Prison Records, State Records Office.

[15] The bishop's letter was included as an enclosure in Henderson's half-yearly report, 27 July 1852.

[16] Henderson's third half-yearly report, 1 March 1852.

[17] Dixon's note can be found in Superintendent's correspondence for that year.

[18] Janet Millett, *An Australian Parsonage or, the Settler and the Savage in Western Australia*, London, 1872, pp. 65–6. Mrs Millett's engaging reminiscences of her time in York as a minister's wife, later reprinted in a facsimile edition, contain many illuminating anecdotes of life in a penal colony.

[19] Captain Bruce was also required to report regularly to the War Office, and his comments can be found in the printed parliamentary papers of the period and in Colonial Office records.

[20] Comptroller General's half-yearly report, 1 January 1851. Henderson's opinion is widely quoted in all material about the prison, but it rested on his understanding of what Jebb had set down in guidelines for new prisons and was an essential part of the reforming ideas about prison buildings.

[21] Information about Alexander Fegan gathered by the archivist and held in the Fremantle Prison collection.

[22] Royal Engineers' half-yearly report, 15 August 1852.

[23] *Papers of the Royal Engineers*, vol. XIII, 1864. Wray was responsible for the half-yearly reports describing the public works, which were regularly published as parliamentary papers, together with the other convict prison reports. He wrote for the Royal Engineers' own journal too, as did Henderson, Du Cane and Captain Edward Grain (who arrived in 1860). The information about treating jarrah in a colony where there was little appropriate infrastructure for timber, was designed to be useful to other Royal Engineers working in similar circumstances.

[24] Half-yearly Report of Works for last six months of 1856 (written 27 February 1857).

[25] R. S. Burn, *The New Guide to Masonry, Bricklaying and Plastering— theoretical and practical*, London, 1868–72, pp. 399–401. Colonial settlers were frequently indebted to handbooks of information and Burn wrote several, including this one. It is not known whether his particular instructions for whitewash were followed in the prison, but something similar must have been done.

[26] Information about James Walsh was collected by Joan Kerr, the great biographer of Australia's artists. See Further reading.

[27] Oral history interview, Ohtr2230/26 Graham Bean, on father Dr Allan Bean, Battye Library.

[28] Superintendent's Order book, 21 September 1866. Records of punishment were carefully kept.

[29] Clerk of works J. G. Broomhall also noted the work that the convicts performed. He had to provide an annual account of what had been done and how much had been spent or saved. Two volumes of his correspondence are held in the State Records Office.

[30] Half-yearly Report of Works, 30 June 1856. Wray's reports were usually couched in plain and unemotional words.

[31] Jean Beadle was an exceptional woman who worked tirelessly for social justice in the early years of the twentieth century. This report has been preserved in her scrapbook, held in the Battye Library.

[32] Superintendent's Letterbook, 1861–65, contains Lefroy's opinion, for which he was reprimanded.

[33] Superintendent's Letterbook, 1869–86, 25 February 1870.

[34] Surgeon Attfield's annual report, 1870. The surgeon also reported regularly.

[35] John Howard, *The State of Prisons in England and Wales with preliminary observations and an account of some foreign prisons and hospitals*, 3rd. edn, London, 1784. His book inspired many later reformers, was reissued several times and his name is remembered in the Howard League and Howard Society, which continue to work for prison reform.

[36] ibid., London, 3rd edn, 1784, p. 467.

[37] Superintendent Dixon's half-yearly report, 10 January 1857.

[38] Comptroller General's annual report, 1861.

[39] Henderson's opinion is rendered in his last report and in the evidence to the 1863 Royal Commission, both in parliamentary papers. The list of works completed is to be found in the Royal Engineers' annual report in 1863 and the other buildings have been calculated from the convict papers, especially from the clerk of works correspondence.

[40] Henderson's letter of resignation, Colonial Office Records, CO 18/123, dated 1 February 1862, comment written 24 April 1862.

[41] Millett, *An Australian Parsonage*, pp. 242–3.

[42] Chaplain's annual report for 1861.

[43] *The Inquirer and Commercial News*, 5 December 1866. Manning's triumph is also recorded in the convict records.

[44] *Perth Gazette and WA Times*, 12 February 1869.

[45] WA Votes and Proceedings 1875–76, 8 December 1875.

[46] Fremantle Prison archives provide details about Martha Rendell.

FURTHER READING

BATTYE LIBRARY PRIVATE ARCHIVES
Convict letters: Seth Eccles, MN1360 ACC4342; Edward Langridge, MN815, ACC305A.
Henderson papers, uncatalogued, Comap 5 and Comap 94.
Henderson papers, MN638, ACC2585A.
Rev. William Alderson, Diaries*1112A (his life in the Crimea) and ACC 1218A (his life at Fremantle Prison).
John Wroth, Diary, 1851–53, MN725, ACC2816A.

STATE RECORDS OFFICE
Convict Establishment records: a selection.
Comptroller General's Letterbook, 1853, ACC1156, C20.
Miscellaneous letterbooks, ACC1156, V1.
Prisoners Property book, 11 February 1861–11 July 1865, ACC1156, V.14.
Superintendent's Letterbook, 1854–55, ACC1156, C4.
Superintendent's Letterbook, 1855–57, ACC1156, C5.
Superintendent's Letterbook, 1861–65, ACC1156, C8.
Superintendent's Order Book, 1864–67, ACC1156, SO9.
Comptroller General's Despatch book 1863–94, ACC1156, C47.
Comptroller General's Letterbook, 1850–51, ACC1156, C19.
Miscellaneous Expenditure 1865–69, ACC1156, V1.
Superintendent's Letterbook 1869–86, ACC1156, C32A.
Surgeon Attfield's Medical Journal, ACC 1156, M12, January 1866.

BRITISH PARLIAMENTARY PAPERS
Most of the reports and some of the correspondence between Western Australia and the Colonial Office in London were published in the British Parliamentary Papers (GB PP) under the title, *Australian Colonies. Convict Discipline and Transportation. Further Correspondence.* They are to be found on microfilm in the Battye Library.
Report from the Select Committee appointed to inquire into the system of Transportation. Printed 14 July 1837. GB PP 1837–38 XXII (669).

Select Committee on Prison Discipline. Printed 21 July 1850. GB PP 1850, XVII (632).

First Report from the Select Committee on Transportation. Printed 27 May 1856. GB PP, 1856 XVII, I (561).

Report from the Select Committee on Transportation. Printed 28 May 1861, GB PP, vol. XIII, p.505, (286).

Report of the commissioners appointed to inquire into the operation of the Acts 16 & 17 Vict. c. 99 and 20 & 21 Vict. c. 3, relating to Transportation and Penal Servitude, vol. 1, Report and Appendix, vol. 2, Minutes of Evidence, GB PP vol. XXI, I (3190) 1863.

Papers and letters from Western Australia, tabled in the House of Commons, GB PP vol. XXXVII, 1865, (367).

Extracts of correspondence from the Howard Society forwarding a Memorial from Convict in Western Australia alleging the infliction of cruel and illegal punishments. GB PP vol. XLVIII 1867–68 (482).

'Correspondence relative to the discontinuance of transportation' GB PP vol. XXXVII, 1865 (3424).

WESTERN AUSTRALIAN PARLIAMENTARY PAPERS
Report of the Commission appointed to Inquire into the Penal System of the Colony, 1899, *Votes and Proceedings*, vol. 1, 1899 paper 16.

SECONDARY SOURCES

Amos, Keith, *The Fenians in Australia, 1865 to 1880*, University of New South Wales, Sydney, 1988.

Barry, John Vincent, *Alexander Maconochie of Norfolk Island: a study of a pioneer in penal reform*, OUP, Melbourne, 1958.

Bateson, Charles, *The Convict Ships 1787–1868*, Brown, Son & Ferguson Ltd, Glasgow, 1959.

Bentham, Jeremy, *The Panopticon writings*, edited and introduced by Miran Bozonvic, Verso, London, 1995.

Berryman, Ian (ed.), *Swan River Letters*, vol. 1, Swan River Press, Perth, 2002.

Birman, Wendy, 'Edmund Henderson', *Australian Dictionary of Biography*, vol. 4, MUP, Carleton, 1972.

Bolton, Geoffrey et al (eds), *The Wollaston Journals*, 2 vols, UWAP, Nedlands, 1991–92.

Bolton, Geoffrey, and Gregory, Jenny, *Claremont, a history*, UWAP, Nedlands, 1999.

Bourke, Michael J., *On the Swan: a history of the Swan District, Western Australia*, UWAP, Nedlands, for Swan Shire Council, 1987.

Brand, Ian, *The Convict Probation System: Van Diemen's Land 1839–1854*, Blubber Head Press, Hobart, 1990.

Briggs, John et al, *Crime and Punishment in England: an introductory history*, London University College Press, London, 1966.

Broomhall, F. H., *The Veterans: a history of the Enrolled Pensioner Force in Western Australia 1850–1880*, 2 vols, published by the author, East Perth, 1975–76, reissued Hesperian Press, Carlisle, 1989.

Burn, R. S., *The New Guide to Masonry, Bricklaying and Plastering—theoretical and practical*, published piecemeal London, 1868–72.

Campbell, R. McK., *The Fremantle Prison: a report on its past, present and future*, published for the Department of Urban and Regional Development and Fremantle City Council, 1975.

Dictionary of National Biography, 'Edmund Henderson', Supplement 2, Smith, Elder, London, 1912.

Dowson, John, *Old Fremantle*, UWAP, Nedlands, 2003.

Du Cane, Colonel Sir E. F., *The Punishment and Prevention of Crime*, Macmillan, London, 1885.

Elliott, Ian, *Moondyne Joe, the man and the myth*, UWAP, Nedlands, 1978.

Erickson, Rica, *Dictionary of Western Australians, 1829–1914*, vol. 3, 1850–68, UWAP, Nedlands, 1979.

——(ed.), *The Brand on his coat: biographies of some Western Australian convicts*, UWAP, Nedlands, 1983.

——'What it was to be an ex-convict in Western Australia', *Westerly*, vol. 30, no. 3, Sept. 1985, UWAP, Nedlands.

——*The Bride Ships: experiences of immigrants arriving in Western Australia 1849–89*, Hesperian Press, Carlisle, 1992.

Erickson, Rica, and O'Mara, Gillian, *Convicts in Western Australia, 1850–87*, UWAP, Nedlands, 1994.

Evans, A. G., *Fanatic Heart: a life of John Boyle O'Reilly 1844–90*, UWAP, Nedlands, 1997.

Evans, Robin, *The Fabrication of Virtue*: *English Prison architecture 1750–1840*, CUP, Cambridge, 1982.

Foucault, Michel, *Discipline and Punish: the birth of the prison*, Allen Lane, London, 1977.

Frost, Alan, *Botany Bay mirages: illusions of Australia's convict beginnings*, MUP, Melbourne, 1994.

Garland, David, *Punishment and Modern Society: a study in social theory*, Clarendon Press, Oxford, (1990), 1991.

Gatrell, V. A. C., *The Hanging Tree: execution and the English people 1770–1868*, OUP, Oxford and New York, 1994.

Gill, Andrew, 'The mid-wife and the grave-digger: Joshua Jebb and the Western Australian convict system', paper written for the Fremantle

Prison Conservation and Future Use project, Perth, 1989.

——*Forced labour for the west: Parkhurst convicts 'apprenticed' in Western Australia 1842–51*, 2nd edn, Blatellae Books, Maylands, 1997.

Haines, Robin F., *Emigration and the labouring poor: Australian recruitment in Britain and Ireland, 1831–60*, Macmillan, London, 1997.

Hasluck, Alexandra, *Portrait with background: a life of Georgiana Molloy*, OUP, Melbourne, 1955.

——*Unwilling Emigrants: a study of the convict period in Western Australia*, OUP, Melbourne, 1959.

——*Thomas Peel of Swan River*, OUP, Melbourne, 1965.

——*Royal Engineer: a life of Edmund Du Cane*, Angus and Robertson, Sydney, 1973.

Hibbert, Christopher, *The roots of evil: a social history of crime and punishment*, Weidenfeld and Nicholson, London, 1963.

Howard, John, *The State of Prisons in England and Wales with preliminary observations and an account of some foreign prisons and hospitals*, London, 3rd edn, 1784.

Ignatieff, Michael, *A Just Measure of Pain: the Penitentiary in the Industrial Revolution 1750–1850*, Macmillan, London, 1977.

Jebb RE, Major Joshua, 'On the construction and ventilation of prisons', *Papers of the Royal Engineers*, vol. VII, London, 1845.

Kerr, James Semple, *Design for Convicts*, Library of Australian History, Sydney, 1984.

——*Out of Sight, Out of mind: Australia's places of confinement 1788–1988*, S. H. Irwin Gallery in Association with the Australian Bicentennial authority, Sydney, 1988.

——*Fremantle Prison: a policy for its conservation*, rev. edn, Department of Contract and Management Services for the Fremantle Prison Trust Advisory Committee, Perth, 1998.

Kerr, Joan (ed.), *The Dictionary of Australian artists: painters, sketchers, photographers and engravers to 1870*, OUP, Melbourne, 1992.

Lenci, Sergio, 'Developments in penal architecture', in P. Dickens, S. McConville and L. Fairweather (eds), *Penal policy and prison architecture: selected papers from a symposium*, Barry Rose Publications, Chichester and London, 1978.

Linebaugh, Peter, *The London Hanged: crime and civil society in the eighteenth century*, Allen Lane, London, 1991.

McConville, Séan, *A History of English Prison administration*, vol. 1, 1750–1877, Routledge and Kegan Paul, London, 1981.

Mayhew, Henry, *London Labour and the London Poor*, first published London 1861, reissued Penguin Books, Harmondsworth, 1985.

Mayhew, Henry, and Binny, John, *The Criminal Prisons of London and Scenes of Prison Life*, first published London, 1862, Frank Cass and Co., 1971.

Millett, Janet, *An Australian Parsonage or, the Settler and the Savage in Western Australia*, London, 1872, facs. edn, UWAP, Nedlands, 1980.

Nicholas, Stephen (ed.), *Convict workers: reinterpreting Australia's past*, CUP, Cambridge, 1988.

'Notes on the Jarrah timber of Western Australia which is proof against the white ant and sea worm, embodying the experience and the substance of various reports made by Lt. Col. Henderson, Capt. Wray, Capt. Grain and Capt. Du Cane of the Royal Engineers', vol. XIII, new series, *Papers of the Royal Engineers*, 1864.

O'Mara, Gillian, *Convict Records of Western Australia*, Friends of Battye Library, Perth, 1990.

Playford, Phillip E., and Palmer, Isobel, 'The Reverend C. G. Nicolay: a pioneer geographer geologist and museum curator in Western Australia', *Early Days*, Journal and Proceedings of Royal Western Australian Historical Society, vol. 7, part 1, 1969, pp. 29–33.

Porter, Whitworth, *History of the Royal Engineers*, vol. 1, London, 1889.

Purdue, Brian, *Legal Executions in Western Australia*, Foundation Press, Victoria Park, 1993.

Reeves, Noeline, 'X—this is his mark: convicts and literacy in colonial Western Australia', *Westerly*, vol. 30, no. 3, Sept. 1985, UWAP, Nedlands.

Rudé, George, *Protest and punishment: the story of social and political protesters transported to Australia 1788–1868*, Clarendon Press, Oxford, 1978.

Shaw, A. G. L., *Convicts and the Colonies: a study of penal transportation from Great Britain and Ireland to Australia and other parts of the British Empire*, Faber and Faber, London, 1966.

Smith, Ross, and Bosworth, Michal, *The Knowle*, Perth, Building Management Authority Conservation Report, 1991.

Stannage, C. T., *The People of Perth: a social history of Western Australia's capital city*, Perth City Council, Perth, 1979.

——(ed.), *A New History of Western Australia*, UWAP, Nedlands, 1981.

Statham, Pamela, 'Why convicts?: the decision to introduce convicts to Swan River', *Studies in Western Australian History*, vol. IV, UWAP, Nedlands, 1981.

——'Origin and achievements: convicts and the Western Australian economy', *Westerly*, vol. 30, no. 3, Sept. 1985, UWAP, Nedlands.

——'Peter Augustus Lautour: Absentee Investor Extraordinaire', *Journal of the Royal Australian Historical Society*, vol. 72, part 3, Dec. 1986.

Stebbing, Tony, 'Thomas Hill Dixon (1816–80)—first Superintendent of Convicts', paper delivered to Royal Western Australian Historical Society, 1999.

Stockdale, E., 'The rise of Joshua Jebb, 1837–50', *British Journal of*

Criminology, vol. 16, no. 2, April 1976, Stevens, London, 1976.

Stow, Randolph, *Midnite: the story of a wild colonial boy*, first published Cheshire, Melbourne, 1967, reissued Puffin, Harmondsworth, 1969.

Thomas, J. E., and Stewart, A., *Imprisonment in Western Australia: Evolution, theory and practice*, UWAP, Nedlands, 1978.

Tibber, Peter, 'Edmund Du Cane and the Prison Act 1977', *The Howard Journal*, vol. XIX, 1980, The Howard League for Penal Reform, London.

Trollope, Anthony, *Australia and New Zealand, 1873*, 2 vols, Dawsons, London, 1968 (1873).

Western Australian Government Gazette, 7 October 1851, Proclamation.

White, Terri-Ann, *Finding Theodore and Brina,* Fremantle Arts Centre Press, Fremantle, 2001.

Willoughby, Howard, 'Transportation. The British convict in Western Australia. A Visit to the Swan River settlements', by the special correspondent of the Melbourne *Argus*, Harrison, London, 1865.

Wray, Captain Henry, RE, 'Remarks on military and convict labour, as employed in Western Australia, from 1851 to 1858', Paper XIX, pp. 116–22, *Papers of the Royal Engineers*, vol. VIII, London, 1859.

ACKNOWLEDGMENTS

This book has been a long time in the making. I first started to work on Fremantle Prison in 1989 when I read many of the convict records and wrote historical introductions to a number of reports for the Fremantle Prison Conservation and Future Use project directed by architect Ralph Hoare. Under Gerry MacGill's guidance, I established a data base of information which has since proved invaluable to me and to many researchers. After the prison closed in 1991, the conservation work began and I met some inspiring curators who encouraged me to keep thinking about the history of this huge establishment. I owe a good deal to Josephine Wilson, Anne Brake and my co-worker, Erica Harvey, who read my words and consulted with me over a period of years. The present prison administration led by Graeme Gammie has been equally helpful, and I want to thank Rob Besford, Sandra Murray, Margaret McPherson and Beres Coley for their assistance and enthusiasm. Many of the illustrations come from the prison collection that is now fulfilling the promise it always held of becoming a place for serious research.

My thanks go also to Andrew Gill, an indefatigable researcher on colonial history, for comments on earlier versions, and to my husband Richard and daughter Mary who have read and reread drafts of this and other books, and whose comments are always rigorous and helpful.

This book is dedicated to Mary Bosworth, criminologist and prison researcher.

INDEX

Bold type indicates illustration.